∽ Praise for *Lc*

"During a long career as high school principal, superintendent of schools, and college president, I have seen endless proposals for improving schools. The reason why most fade and fail after brief periods is that reformers continually miss the point: What changes the lives of students is a caring, stimulating, supportive teacher. One of the most impressive examples is Maureen Ackerman, an English teacher who partnered with students to create an inspired teaching and learning experience. These thoughtful essays by her former students, now in the midst of their busy and accomplished mid-careers, show the lifelong impact of her simple, dedicated approach. This beautiful book should be studied by all who care about serious education."

—Dr. Francis Roberts, decades-long educator and former president of Bank Street College of Education

"Maureen Ackerman is the kind of teacher we are lucky to cross paths with even just once in a lifetime—and especially as teenagers. In this compelling collection of personal essays, her former English and Creative Writing students share how deeply her empathy and encouragement shaped them. Quite simply, she *saw* them. And this helped them to understand themselves on a soul level. *Love, Brimming* is not a teaching guide. It is teaching inspiration. It will lead any teacher or aspiring teacher, any coach or manager in any discipline or industry, to strive for authentic connection built on a foundation of respect and love."

—MeiMei Fox, *New York Times* best-selling author

"Maureen Ackerman was my best student: the most alert, the most creative and poetic, and a beautiful writer. It hardly surprises me that, as a teacher, she transferred those same qualities to her students. In these essays, former students from over 40 years demonstrate the gentle power of her teaching. Like them, the reader will be enthralled by this gifted, giving woman. No teacher, prospective or practicing, should be without this inspiring book."

—Roger Rosenblatt, author of *Making Toast, Kayak Morning,* and *Cold Moon*

"The captivating essays in *Love, Brimming* have touched my heart and stirred my soul. Each one highlights the power of unconditional love in action, and the beauty of authentic self-expression. I loved this book!"

—Marci Shimoff, #1 *New York Times* best-selling author of *Happy for No Reason* and *Chicken Soup for the Woman's Soul*

"A teacher can be a rare gift. In this beautiful set of essays, students, now grown, remember and acknowledge what Maureen Ackerman— an extraordinary teacher and writer—has given them. She asks, 'Who are you?' and the intensity of her interest in them blossoms. As one of her students says about being seen, 'This was the kind of gold that buys freedom.' This book taps the heart of writing and true teaching, and calls forth the best in teachers, students, and writers everywhere."

—Rolf Stavig, LCSW, University of Colorado Cancer Center, Writing with Cancer Facilitator

"In a series of powerful remembrances, Maureen Sweeney Ackerman's students—dating back forty years—recall how her commitment to guiding them to their own passions has changed their lives. As a former college professor in the teacher education department, I believe this book should be required reading in teacher preparation programs across the country. It can—and will—change the lives of teachers and students alike."

—Karen Cirincione, Ph.D., "A Whole Language College Literacy Center for Elementary and Secondary Students," Journal of Reading Education.

"These essays demonstrate that the most effective teaching goes beyond the books. Maureen Ackerman was teaching her students all along the way to trust the process and to trust themselves. Her organic approach to writing, her enthusiasm, her encouragement, and her endless curiosity liberated her students to discover who they were. She taught them much more than how to write. She gave them the greatest gift of all, a new belief in themselves and in a new world of possibilities."

—Nancy Ratey, ADHD coach and best-selling author of *The Disorganized Mind*

"There is a desire in every student to belong, to believe they are being accepted, understood, appreciated, and affirmed. Shaping an environment that allows each student to feel that sense of belonging can be challenging, yet these essays attest to what can happen when teachers encourage students to embrace not only their own potential, but the potential of their classmates, as well. Maureen Ackerman's way of engaging with those wanting to learn is a model for teachers and students everywhere."

—Kevin Walsh, O.C.S.O., M.Div. Mepkin Abbey

"Growing up is an arduous process, and becoming an authentic, whole person is even harder. People often lose themselves along the way and wither, beholden to inner voices that are not their own. How wonderful it is when someone in a position of authority has the gift to stir the soul in a young person and help them see, hear, and believe in themselves. The touching essays in *Love, Brimming* powerfully convey again and again how one person, overflowing with passion, humanity, and a commitment to unconditional love, can have such deep and meaningful impact on the lives of so many. We can only truly know ourselves through right connection to another, and this book reveals the magic of that process. This is a must read for leaders and educators."

—Sergio Baroni, Psychotherapist, Coach, Author

LOVE, BRIMMING

LOVE, BRIMMING

Reflections on Teaching, Learning, and Love

MAUREEN SWEENEY ACKERMAN
AND HER STUDENTS

GROK PRESS

Book design by Mariah Parker, mettagraphics.com
Cover artwork by May Sun
Original cover desk photo by Kailee Ackerman

ISBN 978-1-7337175-3-3
Library of Congress Control Number: 2021922636

Grok Press
www.grokpress.net
maureen@grokpress.net

for teachers and students everywhere

~っ *Contents* へ

⁓ *About This Book* ℃

JESSICA TEICH, CLASS OF 1977

Like so many of the students who appear in these pages, I was profoundly influenced by my time in Maureen Ackerman's class. "Profoundly influenced" is a somewhat bloodless phrase. What I mean is, she saved my life. She helped me discover what it meant to be a writer. She helped me believe in the writer I could be. But even more, she shaped me as a person, as a friend, as the wife and mother I would become decades after I left her classroom. As a teenager, I couldn't wait to escape the world of Cold Spring Harbor High School. But I never left Mrs. Ackerman far behind.

With her cancer diagnosis in the spring of 2017, it became more urgent to hear the voices of her former students across distances of time and geography. When I reached out to so many of them, asking them to share recollections of their time in Mrs. A.'s classroom, I received an avalanche of emails attesting to her passion, warmth, insight, and zeal. Some were devotional. Some were dryly humorous. Some rejoiced in the way she pointed her students on their path in life. There wasn't a student who didn't feel shaped by Mrs. A.'s joyful attentiveness, and by the phrases festooning the walls and ceiling of her classroom. "Find Your Ness." "English Is Life."

English *was* her life, and it became ours, because she loved words, because she loved us.

Like the tributes scrawled across the desk on the cover of this book, each essay is distinctive and deeply felt. They hint at Mrs. Ackerman's indelible gifts as educator, mentor, and muse. Several of her speeches on pedagogy are adapted here as essays, to give a sense of her voice; shorter pieces reveal some of the instincts and strategies she honed over thirty years. With luck, they will inspire readers to care deeply about teaching, in whatever context, and about sharing their passion with others. "*O, World, I cannot hold thee close enough,*" she would exult, quoting the poet Edna St. Vincent Millay, as she urged her students out of the classroom to experience the world beyond. Mrs. A., we cannot hold *thee* close enough.

But with this book, we and so many others can try.

Jessica Teich is the author of The Future Tense of Joy *and* Trees Make the Best Mobiles: Simple Ways to Raise Your Child in a Complex World. *She lives in Los Angeles with her husband and two daughters.*

⌐ *Pen and Ink* ⌐

BRENT PROCIDA, CLASS OF 1988

It's pen and ink that makes her fall in love,
And all the colors black and white can make.
She prods us on with gentle, quiet love,
And all the patience prodding on must take.
She sifts through all our mediocrity,
To find the line that's coming from the heart,
A line that's from a feeling or a dream,
And shows us how that line's a place to start,
To bring our feeling out from all the gray,
To show us that our dreams are no mistake,
To help us move our thinking to our hearts,
And see the colors black and white can make.

Brent Procida is a husband, father of three girls, lover of books, and a sailor.
In his spare time, he practices law in Baltimore, Maryland.

ꙅ Introduction ꙅ

MAUREEN SWEENEY ACKERMAN

You have to find a place to stand.
When he spoke those words to our MFA class, Professor
Roger Rosenblatt was talking about writing an essay, but for
that moment, he and I could have been the only two people in
the room, and he could have been whispering to me the secret of
how to be in this world: I had to find my place to stand.

For years after I retired from teaching in 1999, there was no
shortage of people advising me what I should be doing now that
I was no longer in the classroom. "Write a book," they'd say.
"Publish a teacher's guide. Post lesson plans on the internet."
Trying to be polite about their well-meaning suggestions, I'd
smile and shake my head, all the while knowing that I could
never "stand" on a lesson plan or teacher's guide. My instructor's
words had seeped into me, after all, as had the long-ago
observation of Fran Roberts, superintendent of the Long Island
school district where I taught, who told me, after sitting in on a
number of my classes, "You teach who you are, Maureen."

I'm not sure why the words of those two men have
accompanied me on every walk since 2017, but I suspect it has
something to do with a brain cancer diagnosis and subsequent

seizures, language often eluding me and death no longer an abstraction. Step by tentative step along the park trails across from my house, I've translated Mr. Rosenblatt's advice into, *Yes, I can write a book about teaching, but only if I do it from where I've always stood—with the students themselves.*

But the single, purest reason this book has come to life is that Jessica Teich, a former student and author of several books, has worked alongside me, convincing me that the book will have value, especially now, when education and society itself have changed dramatically.

It would have been easy for me to write about the glories of teaching English and Creative Writing and Public Speaking; or of the creation and life of the high school literary magazine, *Grok*; or of coaching the highly successful competitive Speech team. On the other hand, where would the credibility lie in one teacher's insistence that it was *that*, it was *this*, it was all beauty and fulfillment and wonder incarnate?

No, I decided. My singular memories would not serve. But I was certain that the communal voice of decades of students summoning, and then writing, their own recollections could serve a universal truth: We all, at heart, want the same thing. We want to be *seen*. We want to discover who we might be and who we might become.

So although this book is not about lesson plans for an English class, it *is* about what can happen in any classroom when teachers and students let down their guard and demonstrate trust. It's about passion and vulnerability and empathy, about risk-taking and safety and, yes, love. It's about possibility. And it's put together largely from the students' point of view. That, I believe, *is* a guide for teachers and students alike.

It's also about a teacher's role in asking for what you need, a life lesson never too early to learn. As Dr. Roberts wrote in a note he recently sent me, I one day long ago approached him in the school hallway, eager to request financial support for *Grok*, the magazine the students wanted to produce. Had I not asked, the praise and blame, the joy and complication of adolescence might have remained tangled inside, when understanding was what the writers really sought. And had I not asked for parent support for *Grok Night*, the public reading of the magazine, those same parents might have missed an opportunity to remember what it was to be sixteen.

"Oh, but that was in Cold Spring Harbor," readers might say. "It's affluent. It's beautiful. It's on the water. Just about everybody goes to college. Parents there probably have more time to help out than parents in other places."

Yes, I'd answer. Those things are mostly true. But they aren't everything.

On the first day of class, for instance, kids usually expected to be handed rules. I had learned many things along the way, so it was easy to tell them the one rule that, basically, covers everything: Respect. Look at one another when you speak, for example. If you can't hear what someone is saying, ask the person to repeat it. Call each other by name. Don't be afraid to ask questions. The students, as well as the teacher, are responsible for what happens on any given day, but the teacher has to encourage the simple, yet often foreign, concept of kindness.

It seems to me that basic respect should apply in any setting, not just in an English class, and not just where the student population is considered "privileged." Those whom many would call "entitled" need kindness training, too.

And I'd insist that teaching who you are is the most important element in any room, anywhere. Teachers' own love of what they're doing is contagious. The voice inside a student's head might be saying, "No, I hate math, I hate grammar, why should I care,

I'll never need this," but I have a theory. If teachers are genuine in their passion for what they're doing, if they trust themselves and their students to *see* one another, the transformative power of love is possible. And what a gift it will be to have given that love, even without knowing how it's been received.

After I retired, I sometimes wondered if I'd imagined my whole teaching life, if I'd invented the wonder that I've carried with me. I'm lucky, though. The student reflections that follow are an affirmation that I did, indeed, live a love story.

The best part is that the students did, too.

∽ *Indeed, Believe* ⌒

CELESTE PERRI, CLASS OF 1995

A bout two years ago, I started persistently losing my voice. There would be weeks when I could barely squeak out a sentence without pain rising in my throat and, weirdly, my ear. I went to an ear, nose and throat specialist in Amsterdam, where I now live.

The problem was overuse, he said confidently. I had abused my vocal cords and not learned to speak properly. I would need speech therapy. I would need to learn how to talk all over again.

"What if," I asked, "I instead stopped talking for two weeks to allow my vocal cords to rest and recover?"

The doctor peered at me over his bifocals and declared, in Dutch, "That would never work for you. You need all of the words."

I had been in his office for all of five minutes.

***

"*To Celeste, who has found her voice,*" read the inscription in *Bridge to Terabithia*, by its author, Katherine Patterson. I was at the Bread Loaf conference that Mrs. Ackerman had encouraged me to sign up for.

"Silly," I thought, "Mrs. Ackerman is the one who found it."

In seventh grade, I was not placed in Honors math after transferring from a private school to Cold Spring Harbor. My father was having none of it and demanded I get a private test to show I belonged in Honors. He had tested my IQ when I was four, and, to him, I did not belong in gen pop math, even in this northern Long Island gerrymandered enclave of perfection.

He sat me in the basement for a full weekend and made me do equations endlessly. Every time I told him I knew something already, he quoted Socrates. "I know nothing," he said, supposedly to open my mind to learning.

My father tells this story to this day to all his students. He sees it as a victory in childhood education, in encouraging all kids to reach their potential.

What I learned, actually, was how much it mattered to my father that I was perfect at everything.

And so it was that Mrs. Ackerman saved my life.

When I entered Mrs. Ackerman's Creative Writing class in tenth grade, I had parents who were, literally, not speaking. They had no words, at least not spoken. They were filling the house with a silence so deafening it soaked my bones. From the first minute of Creative Writing, I had a home that I didn't have in the house I lived in. A place to exhale. The yoga pants of high school.

Most importantly, Mrs. Ackerman wasn't going to tell me I knew nothing. And, even better, she never told me to write what I knew.

Because what I knew as a tenth grader in high school was as follows: I knew I was inexcusably fat. I knew that I already had grey hair and that the boy with the big head was always going to point it out to me. I knew my father was leaving my mother. I knew I was still bad at math. I knew that joining Speech and

Debate like Mrs. Ackerman asked was never going to happen. I knew I would never stand up in front of people and have them judge what I was saying and hear their critique. I knew my older sister was smarter, skinnier, and more popular than I. I knew she was a better writer and, most offensively, I knew that she was a junior at Dartmouth. And the surest thing I knew was that if I didn't also get into an Ivy League college, my parents would not be proud of me and my life would actually be worthless.

I would also still be fat.

I didn't want to write about any of that. It was bad enough that I had to know about it, much less admit it to the parade of perfection around me.

But Mrs. Ackerman didn't see an inexcusably fat girl who wasn't going to Harvard. I'm pretty sure what she saw in me, what she saw in any of her students, was the potential to become whoever they were meant to be. She didn't want me to write what I knew, she just wanted me to write. She wanted us, at this threshold of becoming ourselves, to mine ourselves for our own truths. In return, she gave us back her tremendous passion and the gift of being seen. She turned us on to the very possibility of believing in ourselves.

With her constant encouragement and seemingly permanent belief in what I could do, rather than worry me senseless about what I couldn't, I wrote. I wrote like no one was reading me. I wrote like no one was going to reject me. I wrote like I wasn't afraid (though I was! Of everything other than putting words on the page!). I wrote like no one would ever keep me in the basement for a weekend to make me write. While my parents fought, I wrote. While my mother started teaching night school to pay the sudden divorce bills, I wrote. When I was supposed to be learning physics, I wrote.

I wrote about nothing I knew. I wrote about fabulously beautiful women—usually artists—who were troubled, and yet, predictably, saved by fabulously tormented, sensitive men. I didn't write about unrequited love. I wrote about men who pined for these women. I didn't write about my father calling the police on my mother during the fight that finally killed their marriage. I didn't write about hiding in my sister's closet while the police came into our house to investigate. I wrote stories of lives both better and worse than my own, but, most importantly, not my own.

Buoyed by Mrs. Ackerman's praise, her critiques in the margins of my poems, her constant pushing of new forms (the sestina! the haiku! iambic pentameter!) I entered poetry contests that she found for me. Poems of city summers that I had never lived. A mostly fictional poem about the death of my not-dead cat. I started to win contests so frequently that rejection seemed to become something that just happened to other people. With her encouragement, I applied to the Bread Loaf Writers' Conference. It was the weekend of my junior prom, and I was flooded with relief that I wouldn't have to worry about not getting a date, that I could instead spend the weekend with a tribe of like-minded people. That, once again, Mrs. Ackerman had helped me to find acceptance instead of rejection.

I collected confidence.

I changed my narrative.

I had found my *Ness*.

Then, in my senior year, I became the editor of *Grok*. By then, it seemed such an obvious thing that it never occurred to me to be proud of it. I spent the year collecting other kids' stories and poems and binding them. I led critiques at meetings and could feel, suddenly, the tide of peer respect shifting. The perfect blonde girls whose pants were never a struggle to get on respected what I had to say. I was more than just the fat girl with the grey hair. I knew I was still inexcusably fat. I knew my parents were still divorcing. I knew I might never understand what physics was even for, but I suddenly knew for sure that I could write. And that I could write my way out of whatever despair I next found myself in. And then, in the spring of my senior year, I got into Brown, which was the biggest achievement and relief of my life. I couldn't imagine having to admit to my parents that I had failed all of their efforts to make me perfect.

Emboldened by the fact that my biggest fear was not going to be realized, I decided I wanted to drop calculus, both because it was too hard and because it didn't interest me, and also because I had already gotten into Brown, which didn't accept AP credits, rendering the whole process of taking the exam pointless. High on all that I had achieved through writing, I dared ask myself: Why do I need to fail at anything else?

But my math teacher refused to let me.

"I am never going to need to know how to calculate the integer of anything," I told him. "I am going to be a WRITER." He resisted. He didn't want to sanction quitters. So for some reason, I invited him to *Grok Night*. "See something I'm actually good at," I think I said. It also had something to do with the fact that I wasn't good at calculus, at least in part because I never listened to a thing he said. I name-dropped parabolas in poems, as a metaphor of all that I didn't understand.

I hosted *Grok Night*. I stood up in a sleeveless dress in front of a whole group of kids and their parents and my math teacher and said something nice about each of the kids who had poured out their hearts. I took a note from Mrs. Ackerman's enormous heart and shared joy and praise with everyone else. None of it felt hard. None of it felt terrifying in the way I was sure Speech and Debate would have been three years ago. It felt like I was in a living room of my dreams, holding court, free of the silence that ruled my house.

The next day, that math teacher asked me to come to the front of the room. Everyone thought I was in trouble.

Instead, he said that seeing me for the first time as a leader and a voice and not the girl who wasn't paying attention in the back row, "would change how I teach forever. But I don't want you to quit the class. It's like losing a member of the marching band. What grade do you need to get to stay in?"

I was most likely already failing calculus.

"B," is what I said.

I finished the class. I took the exam. I failed it. He gave me a B.

I was right: I have never needed to know how to calculate the integer of anything. But he was also right: Don't stop when something is hard. We are better than the worst of ourselves. We are more than the sum of what we are not best at.

We had grokked.

Mrs. Ackerman's impact wasn't just on her students. She inspired other teachers as well.

★★★

And what can we, now as parents, learn from Mrs. Ackerman? After all, not every student just wants to write all day. Not every student should. But every student should be allowed to develop their passion, be sent off to college or life itself with a backpack full of confidence and praise. The role of the teacher, and of all the beloved adults in their lives, should be to help kids find those things that light them on fire, that make them want to type their proverbial stories to the point of exhaustion. As trusted guardians and stewards of their growth, we should shine the mirror back on their excitement and let them bask in their reflection.

"You're right," I told that doctor, who was both a jerk and, obviously, a brilliant diagnostician. "I need all of the words." And I went back to work, where what I do all day is write stories.

I also, it must be said, do a lot of math.

***

Postscript: In the mining of my diaries for this exercise, I found the following note in a graduation card Mrs. Ackerman gave me:

"And in the articulation of what you know, you will have occasion to influence many. I know you will use your gift wisely and that the world, like me, will be the better for having known you.

Continue to believe. — MA"

At 44, I am not sure that Mrs. Ackerman's prediction for me has come true. What I do know for sure is that the words can be reversed to apply entirely to her.

Continue to believe, indeed.

Celeste Perri lives in Amsterdam with her husband and two children. A graduate of Brown University, she has worked as a financial journalist for 20 years at Bloomberg News, *where she currently serves as Executive Editor for equities.*

∽ *Being Who You Are* ∾

KIRAN RAMCHANDRAN, CLASS OF 1988

A teacher's devotion—to the subject, to the students, to the realms of inner lives—testifies to the astonishing force and influence that define a caring and passionate educator. There are some of us in life who benefit from such grace. I was one of the fortunate few.

Nourished by a ninth grade Honors English teacher, Mrs. Maureen Ackerman, I was broken open and broken free. Her passion and energy impelled me to look and see and perceive, thereafter making me look at everything in life twice. She vibrated with a thing ineffable. She could find verifications of miracles in the places few of us search, which, she said over and again to all of us, is the situation directly before your eyes.

I met Mrs. Ackerman at the craggy and combustible age of thirteen. My family had recently moved. I thus had transferred to a new school district where I knew no one and had no friends. I was a Gen X kid on an endless streak of gloomy days, poised habitually on the edge of picking a fight with anything or anyone that might disgorge the inarticulate howls.

I entered into Mrs. Ackerman's English class first period. Technically, I was not in her Honors class. However, this was not due to my limits or lack of energy. Rather, I did not get into the class simply because I had registered for school too late that year. The class was full and would not yield to a single additional student. The principal refused, no matter the entreaties from my mother.

Mrs. Ackerman was aware of none of this as I slumped into a seat in the back of the room. Very soon thereafter, she tasked us with a short creative writing assignment. It was just shy of Rosh Hashanah and I was swimming with the thrill that was the lack of supervision guaranteed by the High Holiday. Despite these renegade musings, and the accretion of unconcerned, insouciant "coolness" dampening my sensitivities, I could not defeat— meaning I was utterly incapable of defeating—my passion for the writing assignment. I may have written the first few sentences without ownership or enthusiasm, but as time passed, I felt transported by a deeper spirit. Although I cannot recall the theme of the exercise, I can never escape the memory of my total absorption as I commanded my imaginings into words.

The day following the submission of the assignment, Mrs. Ackerman distributed her remarks in the form of that vintage visual: Teacher walks up and down aisles fashioned from a gridwork of desks. This optic always gave me the feeling of someone mowing the lawn and reliably provoking the sensation that I was about to be cut down. Sure enough, my paper was not granted a grade. The comment that topped the first page insisted only, "See me."

Wonderful, I thought. I am about to get expelled and it is not even October.

Once the second to last student had raced out of the room, I tentatively approached her desk. Mrs. Ackerman said simply, "You do not belong in here." There, instantly, came the sound of blood in my ears. My vision darkened into some abyss that put a hold on time. But then I observed that she was smiling.

The joy with which she received my writing was like a river flowing in a time of aridity. It was an extraordinary sensation to be *seen*. This was the kind of gold that buys freedom.

With a zealous religiosity that I had never experienced in any other adult, Mrs. Ackerman advocated for me. She marched into the administration office, begging that I be squeezed into her Honors class. They said no. She was not daunted. She decided that she would continue to pursue this for me until she succeeded, but meanwhile she'd surrender her lunchtime if I would yield mine so that she might teach me the supplemental material prescribed in her Honors class.

I said yes. I was stunned. I still am as I write this. But there was more. Mrs. Ackerman finally got the administration to agree to her request. I did transfer to the Honors class. And I found a certain essential deliverance thanks to the profound perspicuity, heart, and stamina of this unique and magical teacher.

Mrs. Ackerman not only saw me; she would not let go of seeing me. To say that she altered my life sounds silly, but, indeed, that is how the course of a life can shift: Someone pulls you up and pushes you, demanding that you cease wasting your time on farcical dramas, woeful suppositions, and useless wars with yourself and others. Someone insists that you start exploring the summits you might conquer. Now that I have reached the not-so-tender age of 50 years, I can vouch for the fact that there is certainly no room for delay.

Today, I am a writer and filmmaker by profession. I stand proudly in that career in large part because of Mrs. Ackerman. There is not a speck of fiction or extravagance in that statement. Mrs. Ackerman's voice, her tears springing from enormous wells of emotion, the passion and exigency that illuminate her face, and her guiding blue eyes are always beside me. When I am wayward and discontented with my creative process, I remember that she found my writing, my creativity, when I was hiding and trying with every petulant effort not to be found. It is not her voice saying I am good. It is not her voice asking that I persevere. The voice that echoes in my head has no concern with any of that. It is her voice expressing over and again in my heart what she spoke that certain autumn morning when I was in ninth grade:

You are this. You are so much this that I will not abide you not being who you are. You should not, either.

Kiran Ramchandran is a writer and award-winning filmmaker who graduated from USC School of Cinema Arts with an MFA in Directing. He currently lives in Hawaii, where he is an avid surfer, devoted husband, and father to twin boys.

～ *Knowing and Being Known* ～

*Rereading my Journal
from Mrs. Ackerman's Class*

MICHELLE J. BELLINO, CLASS OF 1998

It was the end of class, and we hadn't yet gotten to my favorite part. Mrs. Ackerman always saved our journal prompts for the last few minutes, as if waiting for something to inspire her. While working quietly, I watched her folded over the stack of black and white composition books, imagining that reading our journals was her favorite part of class, too. Every once in a while, she glanced up and our eyes met. Studying her face for a reaction, I felt sure that at that moment she was reading my words. Then a horrifying realization—why did I write that?

Finally, the end of class, and the worry that I had shared too much slipped away. I was ready to do it all over again. She began, "*I'm 14 and…*" I copied the words into my notebook, knowing exactly what she meant. I'm 14, and everyone hates me. I'm 14, and I quit the soccer team without telling anyone, and no one noticed. I'm 14, and I am afraid I'll never be pretty. Ideas were already moving through me, and I could feel that heaviness in my belly that meant a poem was starting to grow. It was grounding, but also a little nauseating.

"I'm 14 and what? What else?" a boy from the other side of the circle asked. Not sarcastic, but puzzled, already knowing that was all she would say.

"*I'm 14, and...*" Mrs. Ackerman repeated, her eyes glowing. It didn't seem to bother her that we erupted into laughter at most of the writing prompts she assigned. "Or," she continued, "*Sometimes in moonlight.*" That one really got people going. I wrote the idea into my notebook on a separate line. The moonlight didn't move me like the other one did. I did take walks in the moonlight, but I didn't want to tell *her* about them. I had already told her enough, so much that I was struggling to answer her casual questions about how I was doing. Didn't she already know? Soon, she would probably call my parents and tell them that I had too many feelings, more than other kids my age. That something must be wrong. She offered one final idea for our journals, "*A secret revealed.*" The word *secret* sank in my stomach like the stones I threw into the harbor on my walks in the moonlight. What made me trust that notebook with my *secrets*?

Once, a long time ago, there was a shelf in my room where poetry went to die. I felt proud writing those words, or something like them, but the truth was I never wanted anything I wrote to die. I wanted everything to be good. I wanted to say something. I wanted my words to be considered, slowly, the way my mother took off her ring at night.

As an adult, I can see the things I was trying to work out through my writing: Being new to the school; missing my best friend who had moved away; wondering what it meant that my sister left for college and came back different. "I feel like I've lost half of her." A place that prompted me to classify my friends into "people I talk to about school and do homework with;" "people I talk to to get through a class;" "people I used to be good friends with and now am only sort-of friends with;" "fun friends;" "sports friends;" and "friends I talk to when I have a problem." The thought that kept me up at night: Did the place you were in and the people around you shape you, or were you you, no matter where you were? The dominant theme in my journal is unhappiness, feeling sad and not knowing why, agonizing concerns about authenticity, and persistent questions about what it means to really know someone, and what it feels like to be known, all undergirded by the fear that I would live my whole life, never knowing these things.

I wanted to be a writer. "You are a writer," Mrs. Ackerman told me one day. I was young, but already excavating my past for stories—getting lost in the woods, my father teaching me to ride a bike and letting go too soon, a carefully-executed plan to send letters to everyone in my family notifying them that I would be changing my name, my friend moving away. My friend. My friend. "Keep writing. I enjoy your entries... It's as if you're sitting here talking to me." Was that a compliment, I wondered? Or did it mean my writing was unsophisticated, too much like talk? I tried to write longer sentences after that, and to use more semicolons.

In one entry, perhaps inspired by a lesson about literary techniques, I wrote about irony. People at school think I'm happy, but inside I feel terrible. At home I complain and everyone thinks I am miserable, but I am happy inside. If I could notice this disjuncture, I wondered, why couldn't I control it? And why did people I felt close to not notice the turbulence inside me—was I *that* good at hiding it? Mrs. Ackerman wrote, "Your confusion is so normal, but your ability to know you're confused and articulate your confusion is so rare."

After this affirmation, which reads now as a kind of test that Mrs. Ackerman passed, comes the entry I remember most clearly, the one about Phil and the wounds he left in me when he moved away. Phil played center forward, and I was right halfback. "We became friends because of soccer," I wrote. But as we broke down the sixth grade gender divide at lunchtime, something deeper began. I was in ninth grade by this time, but I hadn't worked these things out yet. Writing it down, my pretending not to care swung in the other direction, towards "the worst *fill-in-the blank* of my life." I recounted interactions at home, writing dialogue and adding physical descriptions to my siblings and myself as if we were characters in a perpetually melodramatic plot. I felt replaced, I wrote, wondering if things I used to love felt this, too. One night—maybe in the moonlight—I climbed on my bookshelf and reached for the top shelf to touch the spine of every book.

Phil had moved on. He had a new best friend and went on ski trips. He joined a new soccer team, and they were winning trophies, better than any team we were ever on together. I was still filtering things I heard through the lens of what Phil might have said if he were here. It was like that Langston Hughes poem, "poem," which I felt compelled to write in my own handwriting. "I loved my friend. He went away from me." I wanted to crawl inside those words, to be tucked inside that poem.

After that entry, Mrs. Ackerman's notes always followed mine, in script on a slant across the lines, sometimes sprawling three pages. What she wrote encouraged me to keep writing, to experiment with my voice and with form, and to find ways to share my ideas more widely with others. She suggested writing a play, or joining the school's Speech and Debate team, or entering my work in a local poetry contest. She wanted my words to be read by others, but she also wanted me to find community. One day she wrote, "It's funny, but I would never guess from just observing you that all this stuff is going on inside. And do you know what else is funny? I feel I know you so well from your journal…And yet in class, I don't think I know you at all. I wish you'd speak up more." Apparently this did not surprise me then, but it surprises me now.

Achievement-oriented as I was, I was not the kind of student that teachers worried about. I studied and performed well on exams. I never broke school rules. I was lonely, but my loneliness was guarded, well-contained. And this is what is hard to explain, because I felt visible and invisible, all at once. Mrs. Ackerman did what good teachers do—she saw me.

Michelle J. Bellino is an Assistant Professor at the University of Michigan School of Education. Her book, Youth in Postwar Guatemala, *won the Council of Anthropology and Education's Outstanding Book Award in 2018.*

~ *The Power of Speech* ~

LENA KAMINSKY, CLASS OF 1994

I was an extremely self-conscious kid. Now I'm not saying that I was unique or different from most kids in high school trying to figure out who they are, but this self-consciousness ruled me. I felt alone, like no one could possibly understand how I felt. I knew for certain that I was an alien made up of half a Jew with frizzy hair and unshapely legs in a sea of blonde soccer players that, I swear, seemed to look better the more they sweat. I was consumed with my appearance, consumed with fear of saying the wrong thing, and consumed with thinking everyone was onto me as a fraud. I hated my body. I refused to wear shorts and expose my hideousness until after college, when I would finally find the courage to expose my legs to the world.

My friend department in the seventh grade wasn't all that solid after being dumped (my first true heartbreak) by Courtney Burns, who told me on the first day of school that we could only be "secret friends." I was left to my own defenses and tried to find people like me. Theater was my salvation.

Let me note here that our school, at least in my eyes, was primarily focused on sports. If you didn't play lacrosse or soccer, you were a second-class citizen, and my theater friend, Julia, and I took on that role with pride. When, one day after we entered high

school, we were asked if we would be interested in the Speech
& Debate team, *a competitive world of theater and drama*, we said
"YES," in all capitals. Y.E.S. At the time, we didn't really know
what we were committing to, and I had no idea just how much
this leap of faith would change my life.

The thing I liked so much about Speech tournaments and
theater was that I was saying *someone else's* words. When I was
in front of people, telling someone else's story, I felt invincible.
Knowing the next line was like a magic shield protecting me
from my own thoughts and those thoughts I believed others were
having about me. I felt at ease for those moments, and I think
it translated into my day-to-day life. Debate, on the other hand,
stripped that shield away. I also hated conflict, but that's a whole
different story and took years of therapy to sort out.

In the beginning, Julia and I *were* the Speech part of Speech
& Debate, going to the tournaments to compete against schools
with teams of 50 or more people. We competed as partners
and chose a scene from a short play called *Graceland*, about two
middle-aged super fans of Elvis (perfect casting for high school
teenagers from Long Island) waiting to get inside his home. To
our surprise, we won. We won **the whole tournament**. We
got trophies to bring home, which put us on the map at Cold
Spring Harbor High School. Trophies were everything there,
tangible proof of our success. I think there was even a morning
announcement about our win. We were off! We wanted more
competition and prizes and recognition and success.

Mrs. Ackerman volunteered to be our chaperone and would
soon become our coach, while Mr. Healy coached the debaters.
Well, actually, she was first and foremost our Creative Writing
teacher. We loved her. Her classroom, H-17, was a haven of
creativity. Here was a teacher who encouraged our dramatic flair
and accepted us for who we were. We never felt judged. We sat
in a *circle* in her class, which at the time seemed radical. We could

really *see* each other, and it forced us to listen in a way that was not happening in any other class. It was magic. Time stopped in that room. Or maybe I just stopped feeling like an alien. Or maybe, *maybe,* I was meeting others just like me, where our truest selves came out and we connected.

Mrs. Ackerman became our champion. Our energy and sheer drive to be taken seriously fueled us. We would stay after school and practice in front of Mrs. A. She would be on the edge of her seat. Literally. I remember her breathing with us and living each moment as we performed monologues from plays like *Shirley Valentine,* where I played a middle-aged British woman (obviously) having a midlife crisis. I was committed. And as we became more passionate and more successful, other students became interested, too.

We were starting a Speech revolution! We were pioneers in a world that we all discovered together, and Mrs. Ackerman was with us each step of the way. Misfits and outcasts joined our team, and once they found their category, they soared. Fit in. Flourished. And looking back on it, I like to think that Mrs. Ackerman did, too. We all did together. She was learning with us. This was one of keys that made her such a wonderful teacher. She was filled with wonder, and we were teaching her as she was teaching us, and that gave us all the strength we needed to grow.

Then, to my surprise, I qualified for Nationals, which was taking place in Boca Raton, Florida. Mrs. Ackerman and I and one other student were to travel for the weekend together.

You know that feeling of seeing a teacher outside of school? I remember running into one of my teachers at the local drugstore and thinking, "*She* goes to the drug store? And buys things? Like a person?" I'd never been in such close quarters with a teacher like that, and now I was going to a different state? Overnight? Meals together? What would we talk about?

I ended up having the time of my life. One night, sitting in our hotel after a day of competition, we were eating dinner (eating dinner with a teacher!) and Mrs. Ackerman leaned over to me and said, "I love red onions. I love them and I know they make me have bad breath, but I eat them anyway." This small moment is one I always carry with me. Mrs. Ackerman was so human. She was vulnerable and open, and she showed me how to be that way, too, to face the world with wonder.

After high school, I would spend many years of my life pushing that vulnerability away and trying to present myself in a way I thought the world and those around me wanted me to be: Tough and hard and hiding behind who I was with humor and tons of self-deprecation. I'm now 44 years old, and I like to think I've come full circle, back to a place of living my life with more vulnerability and relying on those tools I first began to develop with Mrs. A. Listening to others like I'm sitting in that circle. Trying to eat red onions, even if they make my breath bad, just because I like them. Trying to learn to be comfortable in my own skin, even if that means exposing my heart, (which over the years has been broken and mended and broken and mended) and exposing my legs. I don't hate them anymore! Because through everything I've experienced in my life, the ups and downs, all the craziness I've encountered, I learned from Mrs. Ackerman and those formative years that honesty, connection, and wonder make me feel a little less like an alien.

Lena Kaminsky sings in a band, has a casting business, and is an actor (not necessarily in that order). She lives in Inwood, at the very top of Manhattan, with her lovely wife, Meghan, and their adorable dachshund, Dottie.

∽ *Evergreen* ∾

GUY LICATA, CLASS OF 1996

It was spring of 1996, and I had been spending the second half of the year on campus in the senior commons. It was a bit of a prison sentence, as I had spent the majority of the first half of the year *off* campus. While most of my classmates were enjoying their well-earned diagnoses of senioritis, I was languishing in this purgatory of purgatories—not yet graduated, though not able to enjoy the spoils of the lame duck status I was promised.

Apathy	✓
Latent Self-Loathing	✓
Existential Malaise	✓

A Creative Writing class seemed easy enough. Creativity I had in spades. Consistency, less so.

Walking into H-17, I wasn't sure how things would shake out. I had established a solid reputation as a cavalier underachiever, coasting through subjects I enjoyed (music, in particular), but rarely finding the incentive to excel above a B. I'm still not sure if Mrs. Ackerman knew much about my proclivity for selective mediocrity, or if she had a plan for reaching me, but our time together catalyzed one of the most formative and singular experiences of my life.

Mrs. Ackerman's sensitivity was disarming. There was a vulnerability to her that was palpable, but for an insecure young adult, it allowed for an armistice of sorts. Equal parts muse and benevolent gatekeeper, she had the ability to nurture our flames while granting us permission to be ourselves, to find and to hone our voices. Assignments slowly chipped away at inhibitions and long-standing internal narratives, making room for what she referred to as our *Ness*.

As we came closer to graduation, Mrs. Ackerman suggested I consider submitting a speech for the ceremony. At the time, this seemed like a fool's errand, and in some ways an affront to all things deemed sacred within the associated protocol. I was not a valedictorian, salutatorian, or any other brand facsimile. However, after some cajoling, I agreed to submit a draft—more of an exercise, accepting the reality that I would be gently tapped on the head and dismissed to a list of also-rans. As it turned out, there was just enough freedom baked into these circumstances to kindle a deep-seated idealistic irreverence.

I had nothing to lose.

The following weeks led to my first dance with *furor poeticus,* and the consequent decoding of what the hell was pouring out of me. I experienced the now familiar creative postpartum symptoms of doubt and confusion while attempting to square aspects of both *raison d'etre* and *d'etat*. It was at this time that I learned that writing is rewriting (and rewriting again, and again). I'd return to my corner of the ring round after round, Mrs. Ackerman always prepared with a triage kit to tend to superficial wounds in the prose itself and applying an unwavering confidence to fend off my incessant uncertainty.

I soon made it through the first stage of adjudication by faculty members, and then the second, which assured me a slot at the podium. After further review, I was chosen to be the final speaker.

This, of course, was terrifying.

I chalked it up to some type of affirmative action, or even to Mrs. Ackerman's greasing up her fellow teachers to assure the kid stays in the picture. Regardless of what got me to that point, there was no going back. While I would normally be bracing for impact, it became clear that I would have to double down on execution. That speech became a mantra recited every moment I had alone. The net effect was somewhat of a re-armoring of myself, though in this case I traded hefty plate armor and chainmail for confidence in my intent and technique.

On graduation day, I mostly remember nervous energy being tempered by chatter about which of us were completely nude under our robes. (I was not, although I felt as if I was stark naked...and raving mad for considering the undertaking). When my time came, I felt a freedom I had then only associated with my experiences performing music, a transcendence where one bypasses their standard operating system, and detours are created for long-standing logic circuits.

And then, in what felt like a heartbeat, it was over.

The connection that was created post-delivery was overwhelming, though at the time I processed it more as relief. Looking back now, I see that the content in context has, thankfully, aged well, as a timeless artifact and touchpoint. Since that day, writing has been my secret superpower. Most people don't see much of it, though it hides in plain sight, and I love that. While music has always been at the top of my marquee, writing has been the supporting act and the mortar for all of the bricks in my life.

More than twenty years later, it's fascinating to see how the written word has become so much more intertwined with our everyday life through technology:

Prosaic, longhand missives to a friend turn into a curt few sentences in an email.

Hours-long conversations in person or by phone transmogrify into inches of text encapsulated into small colored digital bubbles.

We slowly truncate much of our existence into acronym as character count becomes the law of the land, the space between zero and one is subdivided further, and our perception of time and space is warped along the way.

The boundaries between the pragmatic aspects of communication and the artistic imperative of expression are sometimes blurred, but mostly cordoned off, which reminds me of a quote from one of my musical heroes, Vinnie Colaiuta: *"Any time you strike the drums, you have to be aware that you're creating a musical event."* Conceptually, this seems simple enough. However, the further we stroll down our creative and professional paths, the more simple (though once sacred) aspects of a practice become more commonplace and even staid. Mrs. Ackerman taught me that while the words were ours to choose, they matter. And even if we feel that those words only mean something to us, we matter.

Since I left high school, I've taken a somewhat predictable path via the longer arcs, with the smaller nodes and antinodes a bit all over the place. I've come to see life as a traipse through a forest with both deciduous and coniferous vegetation, the former offering a beautiful entropy, the latter a steadfast and familiar axiom.

As an artist and educator myself now, I've been interested in the mangrove where a relationship matures from student to friend. There's something magical about that time and place where prefixes and surnames are gently transferred to informal designations.

Although we've only been reconnected recently, I'm grateful every day for the care and inspiration that was afforded to me by Maureen, my evergreen.

Guy Licata is a New York-based musician, educator, and technologist whose credits include multi-platinum selling releases, worldwide tours, and serving as chief drumming guru to Riz Ahmed in the Academy Award-winning film, Sound of Metal. *He lives with his wife and son in Brooklyn, New York.*

~ *Love, Brimming* ~

MAUREEN SWEENEY ACKERMAN

Adapted from a Speech Delivered in 2001
to Prospective and Practicing English Teachers

The daffodils are back, and while I do believe we ought to pay attention to how things bloom, I know this has to be more than a story about how flowers grow. And it is. The daffodils are back, and that's the story of how I grew, too, under the care of an extraordinary teacher whose passion for the written word validated my own love of language, prompting me to turn that love into my life's work: teaching English and Creative Writing since 1966.

I entered St. Brigid's School on Long Island in the late 1940s, and I must have sensed early that the way to survive lay in total acquiescence to Sister's demands. I memorized my nutshells, practiced my Palmer script, diagrammed my sentences, and raised my hand as if seeking salvation after the sin of leftover lunch. And I read what was handed to me, giving back dutifully to each nun what she was grimly giving to me, keeping away from Sister the delicious secrets hiding in the books I was reading with Judy down the street, the Nancy Drews of Westbury, searching for non-existent treasures around the foundations of houses Mr.

Levitt was building in the development he called Poet's Corner.

Twelve years of formal education—four of them in public school, where I still handed in notebooks and still took short answer tests in English class—did little to dispel the idea that teachers were fact-gatherers, not magic seekers, that they did not understand what books could be, so off I went to college expecting nothing to be different.

But there, at St. Joseph College in Maryland, I met Sr. Margaret Ann, Maggie Ann as I came to call her, who welcomed us to English with pages of rules on how to write, reminiscent, for sure, of the nuns at St. Brigid's with their sacred commandments—*no passive voice, no split infinitives*— and just as intimidating. Yet even at that initial meeting, something—maybe the way she looked at us, as though we could give her a gift if we dared, the gift of who we were; or maybe the way she reached into the air as if we were spinning around her and she could catch us, shape us in the hold of her hand; or maybe even the fact of anonymity she demanded so she could read our work without our faces intruding— something made me trust this woman and write, in our first paper, the truth as I knew it at that moment.

"Write what you expect out of college," Maggie Ann told us, and I did. After a week of orientation visiting the Gettysburg Battlefield in high heels and gloves; and after promising to perform works of mercy in the pockets of deprivation near the college; and after memorizing rules of conduct for St. Joe's girls, I wrote the only thing I knew: "Out of college I expect a nervous breakdown." Upperclassmen and other English majors in my dorm assured me that I'd fail, at best, or break my parents' hearts with expulsion after only a week. But Maggie Ann rewarded me. On the day she returned our first efforts, she waved my essay toward us, eager to learn who had written what she said was "refreshingly real."

I was called, I was chosen, and in telling the truth, I was baptized new! I had wanted to trust the nuns from the beginning, but the Sisters at St. Brigid's had seemed harsh and unforgiving in their long black habits. Now I understand that they did what they could, that they were training my memory with endless parts of speech quizzes and sentence diagrams, exercises for which I came to thank them, unabashedly, as I taught my own students the glories of grammar when words are all we have. It was at St. Joe's, though, that the shifting really began.

There I learned to live my brimming love.

To Maggie Ann, language was alive, and in her presence, I was alive, too, addicted to her love of words, intrigued with her line scans and stanzas the way I'd once been intrigued with the greased-back gods of public high school, who never noticed me back. But grammatical construction, syntax, the natural world to be revered: Here they were mine for the taking.

So was Maggie Ann. I came back again and again to every class she taught, paying attention and memorizing things that mattered. I learned every poem she made us recite, I told them to the creek and the night sky, and to this day, those poems serve when I need them as I process what human life involves. Back in the early '60s, I listened to Maggie Ann love literature into my life, offering me permission to imagine the world I felt destined to inhabit. There she stood in her Sisters of Charity habit, her hat a winged thing, while I saw her come from God trailing her own veil of glory onto earth. And on what we would soon wish had stayed some anonymous Friday afternoon, I was watching with her Herrick's daffodils beyond the window, begging them, imploring them not to haste away so soon, when her hand stopped mid-reach and her head snapped as we heard someone cry, "The President's been shot, the

President." On that bleak November day, Maggie Ann had been pleading *Stay, Stay* to the daffodils, and John Kennedy was dying in Dallas, and we began weeping for him and for ourselves and for the whole dry brown earth.

What happened to the country after that is the stuff of history, the stuff of myth and legend, too. What happened to me is in many ways translated into the stuff of my students' lives, thousands of young people who came into the room where *English Is Life* was brushed in a rainbow arc across the front wall, where we breathed in consonants and vowels, discovering syllable by syllable the blessed circumstance of who we were and who we could be. Maggie Ann had freed me to trust myself, and in her name I could do no less for my own students.

I asked them to discover themselves.

I am not simply an idealist to believe that being together with my students mattered. I can let the students speak for themselves:

Peter, who told me, *You made me see who I am. Then you taught me how to write what I felt in my heart without being afraid.*

And Tim, who wrote, *Writing changed my life. I could write what I needed to write. I was never confined. Our class was allowed to chase the words we needed to find so that we were able to make sense of who and what we were.*

And Sarah, who said, *The most important lesson didn't come from a planner. It was a life lesson: Live in the now, take everyting as an opportunity, and don't hide yourself.*

Not long ago, I found an old journal in which I had written, *What I need in my life—wide sky, water, and words.* I don't remember writing it, but of course it is true, and I have been able to fashion a life satisfying those needs. Almost every day I run, and when I run, I'm in love. I'm in love with my feet, I'm in love with the sky, I'm in love with the sea and the seabirds and the lacy foam licking the shore. And when I return, I do the only thing I want to do. I write it down as I had seen it: Clouds touching like would-be lovers. Ferries pledging to pass in peace. Two coastlines waiting like arms, ready to receive.

But if every time I ran, I was forced to list and arrange the main sights along the way and rank them in importance; if I had to compare and contrast the fastflap of geese to the slow circle of gulls over shore—in other words, if I had to take a test—I would throw out my shoes. I would refuse to run again.

Now imagine what you love, or whom, and imagine what a worksheet might do to that love. Most of you would probably abandon it while it's full and blooming rather than watch it wilt and deaden with the drudgery of summarizing, of retelling the storyline of every story you've ever lived. I know a lot of adults who have joined book discussion groups because they enjoy talking about what they've read. I don't know any who have joined book *testing* groups. Why should it be different for your students, for whom you hope to make reading and writing into a love affair of sorts, a way of discovering who they are and what it means to be alive in this world.

Not long ago, a friend and I decided that who we are is in many ways what we notice. Every April for decades, I've noticed the daffodils waving like fingers of light back toward the teacher who freed me to trust myself. In your classrooms, remember that all your skill, all your learning, will not, by themselves, change a life. Your skill has to be informed by passion, by love for what you're teaching.

Spring has arrived, so stop for a moment and watch the daffodils as they muscle through hard ground to bless and beautify earth, transforming its landscape. As teachers, we have to prove as strong, pushing through even the most stubborn resistance to transform the landscape of our students' lives.

And remember Wordsworth, the poet who probably said it best: *What we have loved, others will love, and we will teach them how.*

∽ *Rejection* ᴄ

EVA KAMINSKY, CLASS OF 1990

I want to talk about rejection.

We've all faced it. That unexpected and unwanted rejection from bosses, partners, friends, even from strangers. It can come barreling towards you at any moment, pulling the rug of security right out from under your well-planted feet. Granted, as we grow older, we learn to cope with it better, not to take it as seriously, or at least not allow it to stay with us as long as we used to. But it doesn't simply disappear because your hair starts to turn gray or your wrinkles are a bit deeper. It is always, always there.

In the mess and tangle we call high school, rejection is pretty much one's middle name. And even worse, you are coming right from the cesspool of junior high, where you are basically thrown into the ocean and asked to swim without ever having had one YMCA swim class. I don't know about anyone else, but when I came out of junior high, I was a frightened little mouse. My best friends had recently dumped me, and I couldn't really talk about that, or any of the other panic-inducing new feelings I was having, at home. I wore teal eyeliner and frosty pink lipstick, and I am fairly certain I cut my own bangs, badly. (Is there any other way when you are 14?) I loved and desired pretty much every boy who looked my way and, more often, the ones who didn't. School—

hell, life in general—was a minefield, and I seemed to constantly step on bombs.

But there was one place that was a sanctuary from all of it, and that was Mrs. Ackerman's Creative Writing classroom. The word that immediately pops into mind when thinking of Mrs. A's room is "safe." I was recently telling someone how I was attempting to put my finger on the pulse of what made her class such a special environment. What I realized, after a pensive walk in the park to sort through all the memories, is that there was no judgment when you walked through that door. It would have been easy to call any of the vast mixture of students who filled that room one of the monochromatic labels we give to teenagers: "the geek," "the stoner," "the jock." But somehow, almost magically, when you were sitting in our circle of desks for those forty minutes, you realized that, despite our differences, we were really all the same. We ALL felt scared and shy and mixed-up and lonely. Or sometimes we felt brave and bold and feisty. Point being, you were allowed to *feel*, and you were encouraged to talk about those feelings through writing. There was nowhere else in my world where I could do that.

Mrs. Ackerman—hold on, ok, I'm going to start calling her Maureen now, since I do in real life—loved teaching, and she loved each and every student she taught. She gave her wholehearted attention to our lives and let us be ourselves, asked us to *accept* ourselves, if only for a minute or two. To think that I read my bad poetry out loud in a class full of my peers on a regular basis and only felt empowered by it was a true gift. And it still is.

The reason I was thinking about rejection is that I'm in the arts. I make my living as an actor full-time, and I deal with professional rejection every day. I don't get a job and have it for years. I get a job, have it for a day, and then need to find the next one. I constantly stand in front of people and have them judge me, openly and often with thoughtless cruelty. There is So. Much. Doubt. When Maureen asked me what made our class work, why we were able to go to such deep and emotional places together without fear, I wasn't sure I could explain that with any kind of clarity. But this morning, when I woke up thinking about how I messed up some audition and how actually I've probably been just faking it for the last twenty-some-odd years and God-how-have-I-gotten-away-with-it (insert deep breath here), I realized that in Maureen's class she effectively erased doubt. There was no trying to be something for anyone else, making someone like you, or even being wrong. You were just you. That's all she wanted you to be. Authentically you. I don't even know if she knew she was cultivating that, but she was. She did. I doubt we knew it, either. We just knew that fear was replaced by acceptance and love, for ourselves and for our peers.

It isn't feasible to think that as humans we can erase our worries and uncertainties altogether. I am going to continue to face rejection, whether I stay in my business or not. But here's what I CAN do: I can remember what it felt like to be in that room and be embraced and emboldened by my own humanity. To listen and learn from others. To take risks. Sixteen-year-old Eva had moments of transparency and strength in the midst of terrible anxiety, and if she could find joy for even a few moments in the fluorescent lighting and smell of cheap disinfectant, then adult Eva can, too.

I wanted to include a poem that I wrote in high school because a) it would show you what I mean when I say I was obsessed with boys, and b) those poems were too earnestly sweet and innocently terrible not to. But this past year my mother asked me to clean out some boxes in my old bedroom, and I threw away a whole bunch of things from my youth. Sadly, my lovingly-put-together booklet of poetry was one of them. I thought I would never need it—shows you what I know. So my teenage angst will have to be left up to your imagination. Suffice it to say that I had a big heart but not a lot of skill in the poetry department. Regardless, Maureen made me feel like a Nobel Laureate. I am lucky that I found that class and I am even luckier that Maureen taught it. A good, caring teacher can crack us open wide enough to let our hearts pour out into the big, bad world. Rejection be damned.

Eva Kaminsky, an actor and audiobook narrator, has worked on and Off Broadway as well as at theaters across the country. She lives in New York City with her husband, Brian, and one child-like cat, Gertie.

Those Were the Days
of Miracle and Wonder

RACHEL PERRI BEDELL, CLASS OF 1990

Transported by the diamonds on the soles of my shoes, I am back in my seat for the first day of high school English listening to *Graceland*, Paul Simon's collaborative effort with Ladysmith Black Mambazo. Not what I had expected. The voices from far away were different, but we weren't just listening to the voices. We were encouraged to hear the words. And hear them we would, over and over for several weeks.

Lyrics were literature, poetry; Paul Simon was a genius, but I had no idea who Betty was and why she could call him Al if she ever called him. Swimming in possibility, we eventually started our own composition after wearing thin the spooled cassette tape. What would we write? Anything, it seemed, was possible. Not just possible, but possibly amazing prose. Here was a teacher who believed in us. Her enthusiasm for our ideas was almost worrying. Were we really all the next incredible American author? We didn't get off easy, though. Revisions had to be made, feelings felt, stories shown, not told. We needed to GROK.

We were allowed to fail—encouraged to take risks—be brave with our writing, a courage that lasted beyond H-17. In tenth grade, one student's essay response to Maya Angelou's *I Know Why the Caged Bird Sings* wasn't an essay at all; it was a fictitious letter from Angelou to her momma. And when the writer reached his valediction, "Godspeed," I silently marveled at the beauty—of the prose, and of his alternative idea. We had left Mrs. Ackerman's English class, but we hadn't forgotten how to be brave with our thoughts and our words.

We could write what we knew, but also what we didn't know. We should explore new writers, musicians, run in the rain, fall in love. As she told stories of past students, she would reveal their words to us. "Listen to this…wasn't that amazing?" She made you believe your words would someday make it to the ears of younger students, too. An oral history of Cold Spring Harbor High School.

With her tutelage, lacrosse players became poets, drummers, lead singers, and literary magazine editors. It was a small school. Maybe she knew that we all had to do it all, and she wanted us to be comfortable with what *all* means.

I bristled at times at her desire to know about my life; it could feel invasive, and no other teachers really put themselves out there that way. Did the beauty of our stories really make her cry? Yet her fierce conviction that I had talent buoyed me, and I soaked it all up. It raised the quality of my work. As a high school student, I didn't appreciate what her support meant, but as an adult and parent, I am thankful. We had a safe space to bare our souls, test out a new idea, collaborate, fall in love, and learn to avoid the passive voice.

Godspeed, Maureen.

Rachel Perri Bedell is a public health consultant and educator who writes about caring for parents with dementia at remindingourparents.com. *She and her husband, Jeff, live in Arlington, Virginia, where they are trying to foster their children's appreciation for singer-songwriters like Paul Simon.*

⌒ *Past Lives* ⌒

BARRY C. NELSON, CLASS OF 1996

The other day, I was randomly listening to a favorite song of mine, "Past Lives," by BØRNS. "Past Lives" has always felt peculiar, and I could never pin down what the song made me feel.

"Past Lives" has whimsy...and *wonder*. Utterly sincere, defenseless, *dumbfounding* wonder. And that, I realized (not for the first time; perhaps "remembered"), was what made Mrs. Ackerman's room so special and unlike any other place in high school.

Mrs. Ackerman's difference was stunningly clear from the moment you walked in on the first day of school, and it never left, and you never got fully used to it, and it sometimes felt a little weird, almost uncomfortable, maybe even embarrassing...but you always wanted to be around it.

She was utterly sincere, wide-eyed with this need to convey, with this assumption that we were all with her all the way, comrades. Soulmates, even, maybe. It made her seem incredibly vulnerable, like someone walking around with a bit of ketchup on their shirt, or a "kick me" sign.

There were other teachers who attempted comradeship, like a willful exercise. Good people, good teachers, for sure. There was no dearth of attempts at relating to us silly, malleable teenage train wrecks. That's probably Teaching 101: Relate to your students!

There was, however, a dearth of authority figures who were as wild as we all knew ourselves to be. Teachers who were like teenagers with their defenses down. Teachers who were like teenagers who'd never even *considered* the utility of *having* defenses. Teachers who *were* this way; not an act, but a simple expression of self. Teachers who, basically, weren't so much *teachers* as they were *people*. Mrs. Ackerman was an English teacher, so her medium was words and stories and plays and so on, but you could apply this to anything. What if a history teacher had conveyed to us why he felt inspired by some historical event? What if a math teacher had conveyed to us why the quadratic equation was pure awesomeness? Better yet: What if they didn't need to "convey" any of that stuff? What if it was just obvious?

Like, if you were to watch me listen to "Past Lives," I wouldn't need to convince you that I enjoy it. My enjoyment would be unmistakable.

Mrs. Ackerman's raw enthusiasm was similarly unmistakable. Saying there was no artifice to it is understating it; everything she shared with us gave her *chills*. I know this. I saw this. We all did, all of which made Mrs. Ackerman and her classroom so perfect. I was about to engage—without knowing it, but with that class under my belt—in something she would call finding your *Ness*.

More on that in a moment, but first…that classroom. That classroom! I loved all the beautiful quotes she had on colored paper on the ceiling. All these unfamiliar names, utterly alien and profound and new and just wonderful. Lawrence Ferlinghetti. Gregory Corso. Paul Simon. I knew Paul Simon, sure, but here were brief snippets of his language, cast up there on the ceiling, leaves blown into the room and gravity reversed, somehow new. I was prone to zoning out, and whereas other classrooms provided distractions like the view out the window, or the blackboard, or this one girl's brown hair…in this classroom you looked *up*, your head falling back just a bit, and you let your eyes race over the words, and you wanted so badly to join Mrs. Ackerman in her wild, expressive enthusiasm for them, but you couldn't. Not quite. Not yet. Not in 9th grade.

And at the center was the core tenet of the classroom: finding your *Ness*. Or maybe it was a commandment, or a challenge: FIND YOUR NESS! This was at the core of everything in that room and everything with Mrs. Ackerman. This was what made her so weird and wonderful. She had this fundamental belief that the most important thing was to open yourself up to possibility, to embrace the naked vulnerability required to feel real, real wonder, and in doing so to find out exactly that thing, or those things, that might, just might, lead to fulfillment.

A *Ness* is difficult to define, I think, yet it never felt difficult to define when you were around Mrs. Ackerman. Indeed, if she were here right now, I'm pretty sure she could convince me that I have the definition in my mind, but were she then to walk out of the room, it'd immediately turn to vapor. But there'd be just enough smoke there to remain a kind of impossible but inevitable goal.

Let me step back and contextualize this a bit. This is me writing about 9th grade English. I'm 42. That was a long time ago. If you were to ask me about other favorite teachers, I have anecdotes. Ask me to write something reflecting on Mrs. Ackerman and that room, and this is what happens, apparently. I struggle for a month or so to figure out how to put anything into words, give up, hear a song one night, realize that song is what I'm trying to say, attempt to write it, and here I am, zillions of words in, and I'm no closer to pinning down exactly what it was. All I can say with total certainty is that Mrs. Ackerman was profoundly different, and had a profoundly lasting impact on my life, in ways that I think I've failed to adequately consider in the years since, and certainly failed to reflect herein.

It's suddenly tempting to compare describing the woman who taught us the importance of finding your *Ness* with the actual act of finding your *Ness*; it's impossible, but you absolutely must keep going.

Even as I continue to seek my *Ness* in adulthood, and even as I acknowledge that this is both a rewarding and futile pursuit, it's most illustrative to describe that pursuit as attempted by my 9th grade self. My *Ness*, at the time, took the physical form of a new hairdo. A hairdo change was a big deal. On Monday, you are one person. On Tuesday, you have new hair, ergo you are a new person, ergo you are subject to re-evaluation by your peers. What is this new thing? Why does this new thing have a different hairdo? What does this hairdo *mean*? So many questions.

Regardless, here's the story of the hairdo. It was the summer after my 9th grade English seminar with Mrs. Ackerman. There was something different that summer. I don't remember many specific events from that summer, but I remember its *feeling*. Something was new, and interesting, and electric, in the way that only a teenage summer can be. It'd be disingenuous to ascribe that feeling entirely to a 9th grade English seminar, but I'm confident in recalling that the English seminar played a significant role; that Mrs. Ackerman had provided a critical *something*. It was a *something* that made me prone to embracing my *self*. Not even just *my* self: prone to embracing *all* of our selves, embracing some kind of implicit recognition that we're all confused, all purposeless—*but so desperate to have purpose*— idiot teenage selves. So eagerly disposed to take *direction* from authority figures but maybe thrilled to encounter an authority figure with no presumption of superiority, no certainty of direction, instead wild and heartfelt guesswork, nothing you'd cross out with a black felt pen and write "WRONG" over.

In any event, that summer, I suddenly had all these new friends. I don't *know* where they came from but—and *this* I remember vividly—I suddenly had this certainty that these new friends were exactly as silly as I was, just as vulnerable. It wasn't a conscious certainty, but it was there. I felt it. I knew it.

I worry that any adult reading this might fail to recall how significant it is, as a teenager, to recognize that everyone is just as clueless and silly and instinctively prone to wonder as you are. You can read all the Shakespeare and Faulkner and Joyce and whoever, but if you're not learning that everybody else is just as uncertain as you are...what's the point?

And that summer...it was at one of those lovely young pool parties on a hot night that I got out of the pool, dried my hair, and a girl—a *girl!*—observed that my hair was curly and looked cool like that. Previously I had parted my hair with a comb and slicked it down. It was horrible and, in hindsight, now serves as a useful metaphor. An *actual girl* had *actually said* that something about me *actually looked cool*. So, that fall, I showed up to 10th grade with big new curly unkempt hair. Hi, everyone, I have crazy hair now!

This was a big thing for me. I'm very confident it wasn't literally *just my hair* that changed. It doesn't take a graduate degree in psychology to deduce that my new hair was a symptom of something bigger. I like to think that everyone who had the good fortune of being in that 9th grade English class had their own equivalent: the hair, or the clothes, or the music you listened to. Whatever it was, something changed.

But I worry that I'm failing to adequately describe what this really was. I'd never have shown up to that pool party without this. I'd never have changed my hair without this. I'd have been too afraid. I'd have said, "Well, I'm a dork, and there will be girls there, and a pool, and I'm a dork, and they're all cool, not like me, I'm a dork." Did an English class resolve these concerns? Absolutely not: I was, and still am, a dork. But seeing an authority figure freak out about how *wonderful* some set of lines from a Paul Simon song are—this conveyed to me an understanding, and a powerful one at that, that we are all dorks, we are all losing our minds about a Paul Simon lyric, we are all worried about embarrassing ourselves at a pool party. We are all doing that, all the time, even into adulthood. And I most certainly did not understand that at the time, at least on a conscious level, but I understood enough to dive in, emerge, dry off, and embrace my naturally curly crazy hair, like planting a flag somewhere new and weird, and proclaiming in a shaky voice that this land, or at least this locker, is mine.

But a new hairdo is a metaphor. A pool party is a metaphor. I need to try harder to describe this.

So here's my final attempt, for better or worse.

Mrs. Ackerman was vulnerable, and on your level. No other teachers were. They were invincible authority figures. They told you things, and you wrote them down, and then you were tested on them, the number of correct answers was divided by the number of questions, and you were given a grade, and after months of this, there was summer, and then there was more telling of things and so on. Maybe you were lucky enough to find a particular subject really fascinating. I'd always loved reading, and we read some fantastic stuff in Mrs. Ackerman's class, but the thing is *that wasn't the most important part.* The learning wasn't the books, not ultimately. The learning was seeing a teacher, a grownup, a person of presumed authority, putting herself completely out there, totally vulnerable and open, no assumption of superiority, no "greetings where no kindness is," just another human in the room out of her mind with joy over a passing phrase, or a random thought, or catching one of us in the forbidden act of being right there with her. The learning was the *possibility* of wonder, the *possibility* of rejecting cynicism, the *possibility* of writing something true and personal and reading it aloud, the *possibility* of love. Indeed, even though this is sad, I can't help but be reminded of the final line of Dylan Thomas' "Fern Hill" when I think back on this: "Time held me green and dying, though I sang in my chains like the sea." There was a shared understanding in that room, implicit, whispers. We are green, we are dying, we should sing.

And when I think back on that, and look around me, I am deeply saddened. In my own life there is so much to find wonder in, and I do find wonder in it, and writing this has inspired me to try to find *more* wonder, but...the world has lost something. It's the internet! It's Facebook! It's partisan politics! It's the collapse of ethics! Maybe it's none of those things, but something is missing, and something was present in every atom of that classroom, and every moment Mrs. Ackerman's eyes went wide as she leaned forward and said: "Isn't that *wonderful?*" And for a moment, you felt like screaming with joy, or at least whispering with joy, or at least making a mental note to revisit that joy on your next walk through the woods.

I know Mrs. Ackerman wouldn't want this to be about what a great teacher she was. I get that. There's little utility in a "Hey, what a great teacher!" essay. But what a testament to Mrs. Ackerman's gifts that there are former students eager to write paeans about decades-old English classes. Mrs. Ackerman was, and is, and always will be a glorious, indescribable freak. And the tragedy of this is just that: She is a *freak*. I've never encountered another authority figure who leveraged their authority in the way she did, and the way she did ultimately revealed something about the way we were and are. We never stop looking for things we won't find. We all get goosebumps in response to little bits of language. We all defy and succumb to science. We are all silly, and *wonderful*. We are all looking out a window at the next silly and *wonderful* thing. And if we are lucky, if we allow ourselves to, we talk about it. We realize that we are all right there, right at that same place, where there is no authority, where there is no person telling us what to look at and how to describe it, there is only what we see, what we feel, how we describe it, to whom we describe it, and how they respond, and the hope that their response will give us goosebumps.

That is everything, and that is what I learned in 9th grade English.

Barry C. Nelson lives in Katonah, New York, with his wife, Gentian, and daughter, Cora. He works at a big tech company, and in his spare time writes and produces little songs that please his ears and irritate the ears of his loved ones.

∼ *A Space To Be Vulnerable* ∼

JEANINE MINGE, CLASS OF 1997

Dear Mrs. Ackerman,

Time has passed.
You, my great teacher, let me tumble beyond my own
expectation, to hear my own voice, to know my voice.
You asked us all to listen to the sensory voices that surround us.
Some said, "No, you can't, you will, if…"
And yet, you said, "Yes."

And you, my teacher, inspired me to create change.
You taught me to listen, as you do, to stories and rhythms.

Time has passed.
You are my inspiration.

There is something so very important about our relationship,
about your (wo)mentorship, and the way you gave so much
of yourself to lift us up. Your honesty was both difficult and
refreshing. And the space you created to allow us to be
vulnerable and our best selves was invaluable.

I won't ever forget it. And, in fact, I have worked through my entire life to recreate that brave space for others.

Love,
Jeanine

Jeanine Marie Mingé (Ph.D., University of South Florida) is Associate Vice Chancellor for Community Engagement and Applied Learning, and Executive Director of the Office of the Arts, at the University of North Carolina Wilmington. She co-authored Concrete and Dust: Mapping the Sexual Terrains of Los Angeles *and is working on* Undertow, *a book on cancer and caregiving.*

∽ *No Small Thing* ᴄ

Tara Magnani Gannon, Class of 1999

I have rarely seen greater expressions of pride from parents for their children than the pride I saw from Mrs. Ackerman for her students. There was a complete freedom to love them, a genuine desire to know them. Her praise was specific, detailed, layered. I never doubted her belief in me. She saw exactly who I was and who I could be, what I could do and what my struggles were.

And what would I see looking at my 15-year-old self? A typical teenage girl, one who might annoy me or one I would dismiss as silly and empty? It's easy to do with teenagers—see that surface and decide there's nothing underneath. How many have someone look at them and find more, find their depth and their wishes? And if they do have somebody really see them, one might expect this rare belief and encouragement to remain most vivid among memories.

Instead, I have always most remembered hearing, "You are doing everything and therefore nothing."

One of the requirements in my ninth grade English class was to deliver a five-to-seven minute informative speech, an assignment we all took so seriously that we even dressed specially for the occasion. My time came on the third or fourth day, a nervous, spread-out day of counting minutes and filling index cards, thinking that I would finish the notes just in time, as I did with many assignments. I started my speech. I started well. Everyone was looking impressed, I thought. And then it came apart. I forgot the next part and fumbled through incomplete headlines written in the frenzy of that last-minute morning.

I looked up to the person I knew believed so much in me, and I went from childish nerves about getting in trouble to simple embarrassment and, unexpectedly, to a punch of sadness. She could have simply marked me down and said that I should have been prepared. But there was some way she looked at me, some way she spoke, her voice so genuine as she was in everything, so genuinely upset. More than all the compliments and pride, that's what stays with me—that she was upset *for* me, not *at* me. She was disappointed, but not *in* me. She was disappointed *for* me. Maybe it takes more of someone to show their disappointment than even their belief? To be truly disappointed, you must truly care. And she did. She cared that I protect who I was, my *Ness,* as she called it. She wanted me to live my *Taraness.*

And have I? Well, no. It's been a long time since I've looked much beyond the visible edge of things. I don't even know how to get there anymore. I've been tilling a top layer of soil, and now, trying to dig down, I hit rocks. To actually think, to machete through overgrown weeds of the tedious to-do: It's been harder than I thought it would be. I imagined that substance would just be there waiting for me. But I've ignored it for so long.

And now comes the wake-up call to my own shrinking, to the fact that what I forget *does* wither, does not wait for me like a diamond in the dirt, ready to be dug up at my convenience. I am still getting twisted up with all the *everything* that is *nothing*. It is a thief, stealing from everything that is me and important to me.

Yet, twenty years gone, Mrs. Ackerman has reminded me again. I missed her without even realizing it. But after the excitement of hearing from my ever-passionate teacher, I felt embarrassment. She told me how special I was to her, how she remembered me, and I thought, "Oh, what a disappointment I am." I could not tell her that I had become a writer, an editor, an actress, an artist. I could not tell her that I had lived up to the potential she had seen. I could only say that I still hoped I would write, or something.

But how lucky to have her belief lift me up again. I can go back to a feeling. I can remember someone who knew what to focus on, even if the list of trivialities was long. I can remember being allowed to put down all my stuff and just be. Be excited. Be vulnerable. Be sad. Be proud. Be honest. I can remember someone who cared to protect what was special.

How many children, or teenagers, or adults ever even know they have something to protect? How many ever have someone to help them beyond the tedious to-do of everything?

It is no small thing.

To see the line between all the little things and the things that matter, and help someone go the right way: That is what Mrs. Ackerman always did for me.

What greater purpose can a teacher have?

Tara Magnani Gannon is a procrastinating writer who worked as a certified speech language pathologist. She likes to hunker down with her husband, young son, and two dogs, and write about dreams of normal life at Mom Plus Boy.

ᗡ Finding and Keeping My Ness ᑕ

ERICH EISENEGGER, CLASS OF 1991

Leaving my old friends 3,000 miles behind, my family moved from San Francisco to Cold Spring Harbor the summer before I was to start ninth grade. Having just graduated from eighth grade at a Catholic school, with all the students disbursing to various high schools throughout the city, I believed there would be many "new" kids starting high school on the east coast, too, prospective friends who would help take the edge off my transition. But, as I remember, I was the only new student in the district that year, and it was a lonely first few months. I needed to be strong and find my own way.

Thank God Mrs. Ackerman was my homeroom teacher that first year. Always engaging, she often spoke through the chiming of her many bracelets, like the heroines described in famous Greek folk songs. A month or so after school started, we had a substitute teacher for homeroom, and I distinctly remember feeling some anxiety that Mrs. Ackerman wasn't there. The classroom was a bit rowdy and the substitute was having difficulty getting the kids to quiet down. Probably trying to fit in, I laughed loudly at something another classmate had said or done, and the frustrated sub harshly scolded me in front of the class. There was silence for a couple of seconds until Jimmy let out a guffaw and gushed, "Oooooh, Mrs. Ackerman is gonna be mad you yelled at him. You probably won't work here again." The homeroom laughed, and it may have been my first feeling of connection with my classmates since I entered that school, albeit a shallow one. It was still, at least, some sort of connection.

Mrs. Ackerman was actually my first *friend* there. She took a motherly interest in me as the "new" kid, all the while holding my attention first and foremost as my ninth grade English teacher. It was really her teaching, or *how* she taught us, that's the more lasting legacy. "Teach" may not be the most accurate account of what she gave to her students. She celebrated the books and her students' reactions to them, and she celebrated us as individuals. Often, Mrs. Ackerman was more of a helpful tour guide of my own thoughts and feelings about literature and life, and what made me, *Me*: What she called a person's unique *Ness*. "What's your *Ness*?" she'd ask, pushing us to discover who we might be. "Have you found it?"

I have given a lot of credit to a professor in college who I believe taught me how to read analytically. He slowed my reading down; he had me underlining and notating passages I thought could be important for the end of term paper. But Mrs. Ackerman taught me the more critical first step: how to *feel* while reading. That doesn't necessarily mean carefully reading each word, asking yourself what it means and what the author means. It can even mean reading quickly and concentrating not only on what the characters feel but on what you are feeling with them—connecting different parts of your brain while turning the pages. I'm sure there will be many references to our CSH literary magazine, *Grok*, and what the word Grok literally means— *understanding thoroughly by sharing in another's feelings*—and I don't know if Mrs. Ackerman came up with the magazine name, or if a student of hers did, but I know that that word was a basis of her teaching. Mrs. Ackerman taught you how to read if you wanted to express yourself, through writing or otherwise, and to enjoy it, not just because you wanted to ace the Regents or AP exams.

I remember one assignment we had in ninth grade English, writing an essay about *Of Mice and Men*. By now I knew what Mrs. Ackerman appreciated, that she encouraged us to mind *how*, not only *what*, we read. I knew she liked a more "outside the box" approach to how we tackled our essays. While many kids were submitting papers with the actual assignment title, "Loneliness in *Of Mice and Men*," I called mine "The Lonely Hearts Club." Sure, that seems trite to me now, with the Beatles reference and all, but back then she saw the attempt to be different and play with more creative elements even in the title of academic essays. We'd submitted our papers anonymously, because she wanted to read and grade our work before she knew who had written what. "I like being surprised," she always said. "I don't want any preconceived ideas when I see a name." I clearly remember how, on the day she was reading out essay lines and asking students to come up and claim them, she took off her reading glasses to address the class and remarked emphatically, "You know, I knew exactly who wrote this paper as soon as I read the title. This is yours, isn't it, Erich?" I probably sound like I'm bragging about a small moment that happened thirty-odd years ago, but it meant a lot to me, and I'm trying to convey how proud I was to be recognized by my teacher.

The flip side of receiving her encouragement or praise was the disappointment of failing to impress her. She wouldn't suffer you being too cute or lazy or failing to deliver anything really thoughtful. I recall thinking I was on a roll with my catchy titles, and when we had one of our personal essay assignments, I wrote about Lenard, an old friend from my time growing up in San

Francisco. Alluding to the influence I felt Lenard had on me, I titled the essay, "The King and I." Maybe it was because I'd had too many other copyrighted cultural references in my titles by then, but Mrs. Ackerman did not like it, and it stung. It was not all negative, though. She also said that Lenard seemed like an interesting character, and she could feel that he'd had a strong influence on my development to that point. "You could do better with it," she said.

After losing touch with Lenard for several years, I learned sometime in my early twenties that he had passed away. In addition to the pain and nostalgia I immediately felt, I also thought of what Mrs. Ackerman had encouraged me to do about exploring Lenard's *Ness*. And so I did, partly as therapy for the loss of a friend, and partly because I knew she'd been right. I hadn't adequately expressed my feelings about that chapter in my life. With both Lenard and Mrs. Ackerman in mind, I wrote a much longer fictionalized version of "The King and I," which I called "The Laughter of Crows." I think of both of them every time I revisit the story.

Recently, I went to "Back to School" night for our oldest child, who was now a student at Cold Spring Harbor High School. I hadn't stepped foot in the academic halls of that school since 1991, and my daughter's schedule did not lead me to the H-Wing. As we were leaving the school, though, I told my wife that I'd be right back, that I wanted to see one of my old classrooms. Jogging down the hall and opening the door to H-17, I thought of the many talented and good kids in Mrs. Ackerman's class, people I will always be proud of knowing. But standing there and letting my memories come back, I also saw my closest friend from ninth grade—*Me*, in his youthful, open *Ness*. He was, in several ways, a much better version of the current Me. After you think you've figured it out, I realized, it can be hard to maintain the *Ness* you really wanted throughout life's journey. It's good to be reminded, no matter how the reminder comes.

That night I went home and in my closet found the manila envelope of old report cards, varsity letters, and other nostalgic records that my mother had kept over the years. Back in high school, teachers would sometimes send home "Commendations" in between report cards for students they wanted to recognize as making good progress. There was one that always stood out for me. Instead of checking off the obligatory boxes noting why she was sending the commendation, Mrs. Ackerman simply wrote by hand, "Erich is a writer." Again, I'm not trying to brag. I'm just so proud of it, and it's the only one I've kept.

Mrs. Ackerman knew how to stay with you as a teacher long after you left school. Consider me the proof.

Erich Eisenegger is a lawyer living in Lloyd Harbor, New York, with his wife, Kaitlin, and their five children. He still listens to the Beatles every day.

∽ *Notes on Teaching* ∼

MAUREEN SWEENEY ACKERMAN

L est anyone think that each class, each day, was the best of
times, let me summon Dickens. Some days, some classes
would, in fact, feel like the worst of times. And the students
themselves knew the difference. "I loved those days in class when
we'd have great discussions," Sarah told me, "and you'd be so
proud of us because we all contributed. I loved those days when
everyone had done the homework, and your faith in us grew. But
then those days when some people hadn't done the homework or
nobody wanted to participate…Well, you know what **those** days
were like."

Yes, I remember what those days were like. There were times
when the energy in the room was negative, when the loudest
voices were intimidating to the softer ones and things seemed
to fall apart. An upcoming test in the next class, or a bit of
gossip, or a misconstrued comment or gesture could be enough
to bring the students down. But because I couldn't fall apart
with them, the best I could do was to acknowledge my own
feelings and give them a way to vent theirs, anonymously. *Write
down one thing you're okay with here*, I'd sometimes say, *and one
thing you wish could be different.* Then I'd collect the papers and
read the comments aloud, even my own, where I admitted how

I felt when they weren't right there with me. Most of the time, things improved.

When I gave students a way to vent their frustration, we all learned something. Hearing that nobody liked the nonsense or the sluggishness; hearing that almost every person wished that everyone else would be interested and prepared; hearing how sad I sometimes felt—all of it transformed them for a little while, at least. They saw my own honesty, and they saw my gratitude for theirs when they offered comments like, "I wish you'd tell us at the beginning of class what the homework will be," something that never came naturally to me. I liked to allow assignments to evolve organically from the discussions or from how far into the lesson we'd advanced, but I had to adjust to the fact that many students needed more structure.

I'm not sure I ever mastered that, but I did learn that listening to each other, in the classroom or in life in general, is worth however much practice it takes.

★★★

Classes that met directly after lunch often took time to settle down, so I began reading a poem as soon as the bell rang, not to have feedback, but to encourage silence as the kids took in the rhythms of language and stilled themselves. It turned out to be a calming influence, and rewarding, too, when the least likely student would ask for a copy of what I'd read. I don't know how that would work in classes other than English, but one minute of ease seems a minute well-spent, anywhere.

★★★

A colleague once asked why I interacted with parents so much. *Because I want to* was always my first answer. I was a mother myself, so that was part of it. Usually, it helped all of us—parents, students, and me, the teacher, by humanizing us to each other. And there was another upside. If they had time to help with projects like hosting Speech and Debate dinners or serving as judges at Speech tournaments, the parents were happy to do it. By nature, teenagers test separating from their parents. What a gift to parents to be involved in mutual joy!

But the conversations with parents weren't always easy. They mirrored life, where openness walks hand-in-hand with defensiveness and hurt can trample the most well-intentioned honesty. Sometimes I dragged that hurt home in my school sack, but it would have been difficult to convince me that parents didn't want to hear that a teacher could *see* their child.

When I saw children differently from their parents' way of seeing, I had to listen deeply to the parents' needs but simultaneously explain my personal and professional judgment. The goal was to do what was best for everyone, especially the kids. When I wasn't successful, I still tried to convince parents that I wasn't out to punish, but to teach.

★★★

At Back-to-School Night, giving parents a sense of what their children's classes were like, what their teacher was like, was more important to me than handing out pages of a curriculum that I was certain they'd stack with other handouts and forget. I was thinking like a mother on those evenings. When my son was in school, I was silently charging his teachers with the simple, but sacred, task of seeing my child.

★★★

In Creative Writing and Speech, each class a Pass/Fail elective, the students and I learned to create a freedom that we cultivated over time. Even under "normal" circumstances, some days were chaotic, some made us laugh, some picked at our hearts until we wept. Everything was predicated on trust. I had to surrender "teacherly control," and the students had to use class time wisely to discover their talents without the risk of failure. I didn't know it at the time, but I was also discovering what I was capable of.

"Where did you learn to act?" people sometimes asked in classes I took after retirement. Or, "Where did you learn to write?"

"In H-17," was an obvious answer.

***

I still have a journal from 1987 with recorded proof of occasional despondency:

> There are times when I can't face another 5:00 wakeup or 5:42 bowl of Nutri-Grain. I don't want to be drying my hair at 5:27 or brushing my teeth at 6:02 every weekday for ten months every year. I'd like to enjoy a Labor Day without the thought of Tuesday's class lists, and some autumn afternoon I'd like to be with the ladies who lunch instead of the kids who complain. The routine gets deadly, the monotony of knowing what I'll be doing and where I'll be doing it, suffocating. I've joked to parents that 95% of the time I'm probably asking 95% of their children to do what they don't want to do. It really isn't funny, though. It frustrates me when someone hasn't read a story I've chosen or doesn't want to dig beneath the words on a page. It hurts when somebody complains that "This sucks," when *this* is a poem that to me is no less

than air. That kind of complaint wears me down, and
when I feel like that, I ask myself how I can continue.
Indulging myself even more in the loneliness, I hear
Joe remind me that his dog wouldn't live in a house as
small as mine or Michael suggest that I could make more
money as somebody's housekeeper.

But I also have recorded proof of how fleeting those feelings were:

I guess I'm lucky. I really love teaching. It's important
and it's fun, and I can do it with my heart. Sometimes I
groan about how kids chip away at my heart and wonder
out loud whether there'll be anything left by the time
I retire. But at the same time they chip, they add a little
something, so my heart is always whole. "Oh, you love
everybody," guidance counselors say when they read letters
of recommendation I've written for seniors. I always
believe there's a judgment there about my ability to assess
character, but the truth is I do love my students, and I love
my subject, too. I would have to leave teaching if I didn't.

Here's what I know: It's risky to care and it's risky to
love, and some Septembers I've promised myself to be aloof
because I don't want to be vulnerable anymore. The risk is
worth it, though. Teaching gives me life.

∽ *Presence* ᗡ

CYNTHIA ROBERTS, CLASS OF 1988

One of my fondest memories of being with Maureen Ackerman is riding in her black Saab, en route to pick up proofs for the newly-hatched student literary magazine, *Grok*. I can picture her blue eyes, squinting at the edges, and her voice, always fueled by a deep, joyous suspiration. Whether she was talking about the page proofs we were picking up, or a specific poem, or the beauty that always surrounded her like a glow, being with her was like breathing the same molecules of joy.

As a high school student starting to paint seriously and write poetry without knowing where or how those creative paths would lead, I encountered Maureen/Mrs. Ackerman as a startlingly vivid figure. She unabashedly broadcast an eagerness to see what "we," her students, would create. The currency in use was creativity, and she helped us manifest it into a form beyond our drawings and writings, into *Grok*, which became a container into which we could throw all our ideas and the experimentation of high school era creativity. As importantly, she created the ground for a creative tribe to form. The value of that time with her as our faculty advisor was not just of a pre-professional nature, a resume, or statement-building activity, but also of an identity-building process.

I write this in my studio, with paintings and drawings on the walls, animations for a dance collaboration on my laptop, and over decades of teaching at a dynamic liberal arts college as my experience. I've now spent hours, days, and years investing in the next generation of artists. It is an honor to teach. Not every student will continue on to become a studio artist, but all have powerful wells of creativity, and some will be in professions not yet created by technology, industry, or individuals. During my time with them, I have a chance to help these people visualize their ideas and make them manifest.

I hope I am able to offer my students a glimmer of what Maureen offered us at Cold Spring Harbor High School: that they are *seen*. That their nexus of delicate and strong creative intentions is brought to life, refined, heard. Any artist needs to develop his or her own work, but also to have it seen at crucial times in your life, and to receive in response not only active feedback, but the reflection of the entire universe of possibility in your teacher's eyes: She believes in you, your light, and your creative soul.

To students everywhere, may this volume be an activation of your own work, the urgent, the playful, the meaningful. Mrs. Ackerman would exclaim with joy if she could see it, and she would speak your name, and you would know that someone sees your light.

Cynthia Roberts is a professional artist and college arts professor. She and her husband have been living at their "remote location" in upstate New York, an old farmhouse built in 1866, where she loves tending 13 acres of extensive gardens.

꩜ *Giving and Receiving* ꩜

BRIAN McGOVERN, CLASS OF 1980

How is it possible that a poem could make someone cry? I don't remember who read the poem out loud or the content of the poem itself, but I do remember Mrs. Ackerman, my English teacher, fully absorbed in the entire experience and unabashedly crying. Admittedly, I did not pay attention to the poem when I witnessed the tears because I was now preoccupied by this most unusual turn of events. There were very few things that would bring me to tears, and a poem was not among them. To me, crying was a sign of weakness, a chink in the armor, and not only was I now witnessing it here in a classroom, we were then discussing the poem, and the weeping, together. Mrs. Ackerman said the words "danced off the page." I was completely lost, but I also began wondering if it was possible to re-wire myself and appreciate a poem as my teacher did. If it could be willed, I was the perfect person to accomplish it.

I was uncomfortable, yet I was also interested. Who *was* this woman? In my mind, there was definitely something wrong, but I didn't know if it was wrong with *her* or with *me*. I would study her, I decided, and really listen to her, and if it was just a ploy to trick my interest, I didn't care. She had my attention, and I would construct the poetry folder she was assigning and make both of us proud. I selected poems from various books that resonated with my "expressive" side and threw myself wholeheartedly into the project. I locked myself in my room. I lived through my first all-nighter. I wanted the folder to be a true representation of me in content, presentation, and feel. Her approval and acceptance were important to me, and I wanted, almost *needed*, to prove to her that I was engaged, listening, learning, and trying to be more like her. I loved her enthusiasm for her students and writing, and I wanted to know if I could care as much as she did.

That poetry folder is sitting on my desk 48 years later with Mrs. Ackerman's note of enthusiasm: "Don't you just love having something to be proud of?" Yes, I still say. Yes.

Over the decades, I've thought about what made Mrs. Ackerman different from the forty or so other teachers I had in high school, what she said or did that was so contagious – what separates any teacher anywhere from others in a given school. Quite simply, it was her passion. She had a passion for language, for the bond that could form between writer and reader. She made me believe that this bond was special and unique and that it was mine and that I should embrace it. How lucky was she to teach and share her passion to an impressionable group of students? She was the perfect spokesperson, and I was apparently the perfect listener.

But at 13, I had already defined myself as a math person, more comfortable with numbers than with words, which I've actually continued to be. I'd assumed that was how I was wired. In my mind, most tasks led step-by-step to a prescribed finished product, whether an academic project (get an A) or an athletic event (win the game). It even went as deep as getting approval from my mom for maintaining a very clean room or from my dad for mowing the lawn perfectly. The message in this classroom was different, though. This classroom was not neat and tidy. I was not being judged only by a finished product. I was being asked, shown, taught to delve deeper into myself.

While I believed I could not change who I was, I allowed myself to go further into who I might be. I was skeptical at first, but the repeated message and examples slowly changed my mind. I eventually realized that taking a risk here was not dangerous in any way. I would not be humiliated, personally or publicly. I was guaranteed that the only outcomes were to grow as a student and individual. Mrs. Ackerman promised me safety and guidance on the journey, and I implicitly trusted her. As time progressed, I ventured further into deeper waters. True to her word, the lifeline was always present, and I tested it often. The deal was sealed with the most sincere smile I'd ever known. I was willing to accept being uncomfortable as long as she watched over me.

Motivational forces—the question of whether one is driven by the desire to succeed or the fear of failure—have intrigued me for a long time. For me, it has always been the fear of failure and all the negative feelings associated with it, something I've had to wrestle with my entire life. The problem with this attitude is that it inherently limits your desire for growth. Every undertaking carries with it the possibility of failure, which can be debilitating. But Mrs. Ackerman's class was constructed around the desire to succeed—to succeed in learning about yourself. The message was constant: You cannot fail if you risk discovering your capabilities. This required a leap of faith and more energy than I was used to giving, but because it was presented to her students as almost certain success, I came to consider, why not? I began to understand that the poetry project I'd initially seen as a task had actually turned into a journey, a brilliant journey that expanded my limits of expression, self-confidence, and pride. It turned out to be a gift to myself.

But I would give her a gift, too, a part of myself that she knew was hidden. Initially, I didn't know it or believe it, and when I finally came to believe her, I didn't know how to find what she saw. She helped me find it, though, through an experience that turned out to be so much more than pasting poems into a folder. It was my gift to both of us.

Now I am a doctor, and I listen to patients' stories, and, in turn, I talk to them as candidly and humanly as possible. People listen to doctors, trusting that they will tell the truth. I want people to listen to this story I'm telling, this true story of giving and receiving—my story of faith and trust and self-reflection.

Brian McGovern, an emergency physician and father of five sons, lives in Wilton, Connecticut. After playing soccer and lacrosse at Princeton, he has been team physician for the USA Lacrosse Team and the USA Wrestling Team and has coached more than 60 teams in various sports at the youth and high school level.

◇ *The Full Mausie* ◇

Bill Danon, Class of 1991

I never became the writer I thought I would when I left Mrs. Ackerman's ninth grade classroom.

I had come into her English class a mutable, unformed adolescent. I was a good student and a sensitive kid, but not overly so. I played sports, though not the high-status ones in Cold Spring Harbor—lacrosse and soccer. I trash-talked with the other boys. I snuck out of the house at night, through a window and down a drainpipe. I had a fleeting sense of myself as an engineer after making a third-place contraption out of a mouse-trap and old vinyl forty-fives for a physics contest.

I did not see myself as a writer in September of that year, and certainly not as a writer of poetry. But somehow, by June, I felt as if a previously unexpressed writer's chromosome had been turned on.

After Mrs. Ackerman, I wrote poetry through college and into adulthood. It was unrefined, but it wasn't unserious. It even helped woo my wife. When I was able to write a perfect line or two, the almost magical sequence of words that captured a mood, a scene, an experience in a fresh and precise way, I felt more human and alive. But I haven't kept it up, and it never became the vocation I imagined as a real possibility by the end of ninth grade. Rightly so,

I think. It wasn't—and isn't—the whole me. But it's a deep part of how I see myself and how I see the world.

It seems to me now entirely plausible that I could have missed this writerly nature. The gene was there, but it took Mrs. Ackerman—Mausie, as I later came to call her—to expose and cultivate it. Without her, I'm sure I would still love books, but I may have preferred the tenacity of good nonfiction to the hard-earned invention of good fiction. I wouldn't have the same admiration of well-crafted language, like Angela Carter's simile for an old curmudgeon whose demeanor was "grim as a prison dinner." And, most importantly, I wouldn't observe life with the same sociological eye, looking for meaning in the way people behave on the street, at a school playground, in a bar at happy hour—and the right words to capture it.

How did Mrs. Ackerman help me and so many other students come to understand themselves (find their *Ness*, in her parlance)?

It seems to me it was a rare but not complicated mixture of enthusiasm and expectations. Mrs. Ackerman gave so much of herself to her students. She was unfalteringly generous with her time, her praise, her on-the-nose critiques, her love. She was soft-hearted, but not soft. Her demands were firm.

She could gush over someone's small observation about a character in a short story until the observer blushed deep pink, and the next day, she'd demand the right punctuation for nonessential relative clauses until an errant punctuator blushed purple.

We were expected to open up our self-conscious protean selves in writing exercises. When we did, whatever we said, if we said it true, she would gasp and grab us by the arm and beam.

We were expected to memorize what seemed like impossibly long passages from Shakespeare. It was a task that seemed old-fashioned and silly. But there was no budging. You'll remember it the rest of your lives, Mrs. Ackerman said, as justification.

That seemed preposterous, but she wanted the music of iambic pentameter to live inside us forever. Of course, she was right.
I don't really remember the grammar (or Marc Antony's eulogy, to be honest), but I can still recite, "Love is a smoke raised with the fume of sighs..." thirty years later.

At first, I found Mrs. Ackerman's earnestness almost comical, but also disarming. It wasn't hard to see that it was real, and there were rewards for letting down your defenses.

The breakthrough for me was a poem I wrote about sidewalks and how the act of falling in love causes you to see the world with fresh wonder. How the history told by the cracks and tree-root bulges and plant-life surging through concrete was worthy of notice and appreciation. Teenage stuff for sure, but newly true to me. That earned the full Mausie, beaming and clutching.

Her reaction wasn't: great job, gold star. She wanted to edit and nurture. The cliche of "warm summer rain" wouldn't do. Even on hot summer days, the rain is cooling to your skin, isn't it? Yes, she was right. I didn't make that edit, but I got her point. You had to take care with how you observed the world and how you wrote about it. *Especially* if you were writing about your love-fueled powers of observation.

It went on from there. I wrote, she reviewed. She was always kind and encouraging, but she would also tell me when a metaphor was unacceptably feeble. She shared her favorite writers, some staples of high school curricula, some definitely not. I remember being dazzled by Sherwood Anderson and (though it took time) Richard Brautigan.

We stayed close during my four school years through the literary magazine, *Grok*. Senior year, my friend Josh and I were co-editors.

At some point along the way, our relationship evolved into a friendship. She stopped being Mrs. Ackerman and became

Mausie. I became Billy, a variant on my name I had shunned since elementary school. The diminutive forms signaled affection, and it worked.

Maybe Mausie was a unicorn. I hope not. I hope the schools are filled with Mausies. All it takes is unrestrained love and unbending expectations. I had many other good teachers and professors in high school, college, and grad school, but never another like Mausie. I guess that combination is uncommon. Most of us are lucky to encounter a Mausie once in our lives. I hope my daughter—a far more voracious reader than I ever was—finds her Mausie and can get in touch with that writer's sense of the world. Of looking, always looking.

I may never have become a professional writer, but learning in Mrs. Ackerman's class to see myself and see the world as a writer mattered.

I said earlier that my amateur poetry helped me woo my future wife. And when my abilities came up short, I borrowed from one of the offbeat pros Mausie introduced. I read Richard Brautigan's "Gee, You're so Beautiful That It's Starting to Rain" during our wedding ceremony. But I adapted the named object of his affection and her "long blonde beauty" in the poem to suit my red-headed bride. I think Mausie and Brautigan would approve.

Bill Danon lives in the San Francisco Bay Area with his wife and daughter. When he's not busy with a never-ending quest to repair and restore his mid-century modern house, Bill works as a brand marketer in the tech industry.

ᗧ *Healing from Within:* ᗤ
How Writing Saved Me After Tragedy

JEANNY KIM LEE, CLASS OF 1989

For the first 47 years of my life, I had nothing but good fortune. Then, one morning, my younger sister died of sudden cardiac arrest, less than 12 hours after we had last texted each other. In an instant, I lost my best friend: the one who felt like an extension of me, the one who had been a second mother to my three daughters, the one who had a two-year-old son and a husband who needed her. I knew that life could be cruel, but this was unacceptable. As I was reeling from the shock and grief, I immediately took comfort in a survival technique I had learned 30 years ago, as a high school student in Mrs. Ackerman's Creative Writing class.

As a child of Korean immigrants who were consumed with establishing themselves in a foreign country, I learned at an early age that my parents were neither adept at nor comfortable with the task of indulging my emotions. They were raised in a culture that regards the display of emotions as a weakness that undermines any personal accomplishment. I had resigned myself to a life of silent rumination until I met Mrs. Ackerman and discovered that true joy only exists in the space where we share and validate our life experiences. There is no other way to survive our journey.

I had the privilege of being in Mrs. Ackerman's English and Creative Writing classes in addition to being the editor of our high school literary magazine, *Grok*. It was under her loving guidance that I discovered the power of the written word. As my fellow writers and I shared poems, stories, and essays about matters that loomed large in the mind of an adolescent, I discovered that I could find meaning and strength not only in the thoughts shared by my peers but, more importantly, in the thoughts that found their way from my head to the paper. It was an eclectic group that made up our Creative Writing classes and *Grok* contributors, students from every stereotypical high school clique, but we had carved out a place where the only thing held in high esteem was the vulnerability displayed in our writing.

I would be remiss if I did not acknowledge the role Mrs. Ackerman played in cultivating an incredible environment where aimless and self-absorbed teenagers could find a "voice" to express their joy, heartache, and everything in between. She was encouraging without being overbearing, invested without being desperate. She was a living reminder that the world was full of possibilities and that we owed ourselves the gift of hope. Mrs. Ackerman was that teacher who not only believed in us but made us believe in ourselves.

But that was not the only fortuitous circumstance that enabled us to cultivate an environment of trust that seems almost impossible today. We were fortunate that social media did not exist to numb or distract us from our emotions. We were even more fortunate that we chose to give expression to our joy and pain through writing and not through means that could be destructive. It was the confluence of these factors that taught us the healing power of words—both the words of others and, as I would discover later on, the words we find within ourselves.

Writing continues to be of utmost importance to me, and it has carried me through all the highs and lows of my enriching and fulfilling life. When I re-read things I have written after years have passed, I am always surprised at how much I learn about myself, from myself. I learn lessons that no one else could have taught me, lessons that no one else would want to teach me. It was in Mrs. Ackerman's class that I discovered that my feelings and experiences are worthy of being lovingly recorded, revisited, remembered, and restored. I can learn more about myself from what I felt in the past than what I am feeling right now. And this was the process that ultimately brought me healing after the devastating loss of my sister. As I poured out my grief in my writing, I was giving myself the precious gift of processing my pain with the only person who could truly understand that pain. Writing forced me to be rational about something that was completely irrational, and my words gave me the courage to move on and believe that I would survive losing her.

When I share about *Grok* and Mrs. Ackerman with my high school-aged daughters, they are skeptical about whether they could engage in such a personal relationship with their teachers or peers today. The culture in which they find themselves does not seem to value the open and authentic expression of hope and faith, which is critical to elevating a relationship from the transactional to the transcendent. Their interactions with classmates and teachers are clinical and goal-oriented: students pursue the singular goal of academic achievement, and teachers seem content to maintain their distance. However, I still have faith that every teacher and every student has the capacity to push each other in ways that are rewarding and life-giving. The most important change that must occur remains the collective responsibility of everyone outside the school walls—those who wield influence over students to remind them that the classroom is a place of true learning, not just "education." Students need to be encouraged to put aside their cynicism and distrust of authority and believe that meaningful interactions can occur in the classroom. They must see that they owe themselves the priceless gift of finding that one teacher who opens up a world of possibilities. I cannot imagine surviving adolescence without a teacher like Mrs. Ackerman to remind me that high school is not just that transition between childhood and adulthood, but rather a journey that will influence the course of my adulthood.

In today's high-stress schools, filled with overly-parented and self-indulgent children, the task of connecting in a meaningful way with a student must seem both impossible and undesirable to teachers. It is easier to keep the relationship transactional. However, despite the technological advances that have contributed to making students insular and inattentive, the truth remains that students yearn for a classroom environment where they are respected for their ideas and encouraged to explore what they believe. The lack of introspection among adolescents has resulted in a generation of students who are not equipped to process the range of emotions they encounter in their volatile teenage years. We need to encourage teachers to approach students with empathy rather than distrust, because we still believe teachers have the capacity to change students' lives. So much of who we become as an adult is sown in our high school years, and I am certain that Mrs. Ackerman gave me the gift of knowing and trusting myself.

Jeanny Kim Lee, a lawyer for an international human rights organization, is working on a memoir. She resides outside of Washington, D.C. with her family.

✑ *What We Carry* ✑

Tara Malone Kearney, Class of 1995

I spent much of ninth grade in a mild state of dread. Not for the normal reasons that might give a 14-year-old angst, mind you—a friendship gone sour or an Algebra class that just wouldn't get easier. These things didn't faze me. But two words scared me to my toes: Speak-Off.

Every ninth grade student in our high school would research an issue—anything from the history of the Second Amendment to Indie Rock—draft a five-to-seven minute speech on the topic, and then deliver this speech to their English class. Students were both to inform and to engage with the substance of their speech and the nature of their delivery.

I loved to read, write, and delve into a subject; indeed, years later, this love of the written word led me to a career in journalism. But the thought of giving a speech in front of classmates scared me, well, speechless.

I had only come to the school a year earlier, and eighth grade is not an easy time to jump into a new environment. I stepped into Cold Spring Harbor High School on Long Island having spent most of my childhood moving every few years from one international school to the next, the perpetual new kid. This schooled me in the art of observation, a great skill that later came into play in my reporting work, but it often left me feeling out of step.

Yet in Classroom H-17, I fit.

A creative whirl of a teacher whose classroom was as colorful and inviting as she was, Mrs. Maureen Ackerman welcomed the dozen students in our ninth grade seminar class with a challenge to create something, be it a poem or a speech, that was true to ourselves. She led us in cornerstone lessons in grammar and contrasting reads of novels like *Lord of the Flies* and *To Kill a Mockingbird*. Through it all, Mrs. Ackerman inspired us to dig deeper, write honestly, and above all, to create.

Within the vibrant walls of Mrs. Ackerman's classroom, I found my voice. Perhaps just as importantly, I found the self-confidence to share my voice with a belief that my ideas and my work merited it. The intimate nature of the class surely helped. So, too, did the smiling, stylish force of Mrs. Ackerman, who paired high praise with high expectations. Add in her belief in us, and for me, at least, it was inspiration to speak up.

When the speech unit rolled around in January, Mrs. Ackerman advised us to pick our topics wisely. "You'll spend a lot of time with it," she said. I settled on the issue of sexual harassment in the wake of the Justice Clarence Thomas nomination hearings for the U.S. Supreme Court and the accusations leveled by Professor Anita Hill. It was a weighty issue for a fourteen-year-old, but the speech came together well. Still, no one was more surprised than I was when my speech was selected for the Ninth Grade Speak-Off. The student who was initially scared to give a speech in front of twelve classmates now would be called to deliver her speech before the entire ninth grade, a number of teachers, and a handful of parents and school board members. In the end, my speech won the competition.

Many speeches would follow. I joined the high school's Speech and Debate team and competed in the category of Original Oratory, delivering speeches that I researched and wrote. I qualified for both state and national tournaments. Through all this, Mrs. Ackerman helped me find my voice. She believed I had the strength to share it, so I did, too.

So steadfast was her support that she accepted with understanding my decision to forego the national speech competition—twice— and not represent our high school. I was fortunate enough to have earned a seat on our high school's rowing team. The top race of the rowing season occurred during the same weekend as the national speech competition. In one event, I competed alone, and, in the other, I raced with a teammate in a double skull. This basic math made the decision for me. I learned a great deal about myself, and about Mrs. Ackerman, in the process, however. Mrs. Ackerman seemed to delight in watching me grow even as my decision led me in a different direction. Perhaps this is the hallmark of a truly gifted educator—acceptance without judgment, trust without condition, growth without limit.

I was one of many students graced by Mrs. Ackerman's gifts. Because whether through words, written or spoken, or creative fiction or non-fiction, Mrs. Ackerman believed we all had something important and worthwhile to say. Students, for their part, carry this faith with them beyond any one class or any one school. It becomes part of the lens through which they see themselves and their place in the world.

More than two decades later, I carry her belief in me still.

Tara Malone Kearney, whose work has been honored by the Associated Press, the Education Writers Association, the Neiman Foundation for Journalism, and the National Headline Awards, was an education journalist for more than a decade at the Chicago Tribune *and other area publications. Currently a freelance writer, she lives with her husband and four children in the Chicago region.*

～ *A Person Worth Loving* ～

TAMI THOMPSON WOOD, CLASS OF 1997

Mrs. Ackerman, my Creative Writing teacher and Speech coach, loved words. She loved the way they made the hair on her arms stand on edge when they were linked together in a beautiful speech or poem. And she loved the way they played like an instrument in her mind long after she'd read them. Like a child, Mrs. Ackerman also loved the world. She understood that poetry wasn't meant only for classrooms, but for hillsides, too. Words taste better outdoors.

I was a nervous ninth grader when I performed for Mrs. Ackerman on my first day in Speech and Debate class. "You're a lifer," she said after my delivery of Mary Fisher's *Remarks on AIDS*. "You'll stay with this." After class she took me outside, telling me I couldn't leave until I had embraced the world. I thought she was kidding, but her blue eyes were filled with an excitement and innocence that I had never before seen in an adult, so outside the school building, with the quiet hum of the hallways in the background, I held my arms up in the air and proclaimed with Edna St. Vincent Millay, "O, World, I cannot hold thee close enough!"

It was my trust in and love for Mrs. Ackerman that convinced me to sign up for Creative Writing class in the spring of my sophomore year. "I want to find a way to get what's inside of me on paper," I told her. And though it took several months of crumpled up loose-leaf and endless erasures, I finally found a comfortable voice, not the voice of Mary Fisher or Edna St. Vincent Millay, but the voice of Tami Thompson, a sometimes shy, sometimes silly girl who wrote what were her best pieces in the margins of her class notebook.

"If I could give my students one gift," Mrs. Ackerman often said, "it would be the gift of reverence." I was never sure what this meant until one afternoon when I stepped outside to breathe some May air, and I saw the trees in the courtyard blooming magnolia and the sun reflecting off the new green grass. I knew then that the world, like a butterfly, can never really be held. What it can be is revered.

Mrs. Ackerman's love of the world taught me to appreciate life in a way I never had before. Her love of words prompted me to discover my own voice, which she then dared me to use. But maybe it was Mrs. Ackerman's love for me that taught me the most. It encouraged me to look inside myself to find a person worth loving, a person who can and should be embraced.

Tami Thompson Wood is a museum educator who leads programs aimed at connecting participants with famous works of art and inspiring their own creativity. She lives on Long Island with her husband and two children.

~ Teaching Life as English ~ and Other Daily Voyages to Possibility

BRIAN FOERSTER, CLASS OF 1991

nglish Is Life across the front wall. *Find Your Ness* across the ceiling.

There I sat, ready to start ninth grade Honors English, and I already had a mild suspicion that this was going to be a little different from other new classes: Peculiar, for sure, and not as demanding. I was wrong.

I was wrong not only about how that judgment ultimately contrasted with what the class was *actually* all about, but even more about what the next four years of my life would bring. Anxiety. Unrequited love. Athletic successes and pathetic defeats. Depression. Hamlet-worthy inaction. Unpopularity. Popularity. Good friends. Bad friends. Excess. Awkwardness. Senior year camaraderie and catharsis.

And then, as everything hurtled towards the graduation finish line, came the dark silencing of a harrowing drumbeat that I'd dreaded, my father's death from the cancer that he had valiantly battled for over a year.

So I can't talk about Mrs. Ackerman, the architect of those mantras and the high bar of excellence she demanded from us, without connecting her to the most important milestones and events of my high school years. That is where Mrs. Ackerman and *English Is Life* are right at home: Creating a world where quality and depth of character matter.

QUALITY

In Mrs. Ackerman's class, you were going to become a competent, if not good, writer, and in the process would develop a more incisive understanding of English literature. Often, that meant you were going to get there sometimes through the ferocity of her pen on your pages. And that was humbling for most of us who had not encountered rigor like this before.

But there was another demand in this class that made it so much more than academically demanding—and that was the demand for quality of thought, which cannot be achieved with ferocity. Instead, it came in discussions with awakening adolescents slowly realizing that there was something amazing happening in connecting the verses of a poem to their view on life, connecting them sometimes to their insecurities or their inspiration. The really brave might relate to their confused feelings of like and love, or hate for that matter, but mostly love. Awkward boys found a place in H-17 where they finally, for 40 minutes at least, felt connected to the world, discovering, maybe, that there was a world of much greater possibility awaiting them once this tortured high school routine came to an end. Or to the jocks it was a place to let down their guard and first dabble in what matters far more than the trappings of high school fame and glory. I can attest to both of these examples as I dabbled on both the awkward and jock teams, often simultaneously.

We were all, as Mrs. Ackerman implored on the ceiling of the classroom, finding our *Ness* – i.e., that which made us our own unique selves.

DEPTH OF CHARACTER

Which flows right into developing the goal of closeness and a comfort level among all of us that would help us find our individual voices. In a twist of dark irony, one of the tasks we had in tenth grade Speech class, a course I took entirely because it was taught by Mrs. Ackerman, was to eulogize someone. I had not known anyone beyond quite distant relatives to die at this point, so the thought was really just to find someone you admired and to speak about this person in a familiar way with stories that brought their essence to life. I chose my father. Two years later, when his real death was unfolding and I, as a senior, was taking Creative Writing as an independent study with Mrs. Ackerman, I was so grateful to have had four years of classes with her as a sturdy foundation of trust, because I had developed both a much-needed outlet for grief through writing and a battle-tested friendship with a teacher who cared deeply for her students, so much so that her initials—MA—became an often-used term of endearment for our school mother. Our Ma.

Once developed, depth of character can be summoned at times of agony, when the choice can be courage vs. anger or strength vs. hopelessness; it can be tested in times of great success when the choice can be humility vs. hubris or generosity vs. selfishness. Mrs. Ackerman only wanted to live in the realm of deep character. I don't believe she felt comfortable in settings where the primary goal was "small talk." Don't get me wrong. She loves to laugh, and she loves humor and the fleeting moments of happenstance that appear to her sometimes with a twinge of predetermination. (*It could only have happened that way!*) But at her essence, she wanted to get down to what matters most, the depth of who we were and who we were becoming.

And that is a rare and wonderful thing in a teacher, something to be celebrated, as much as she celebrated our own personal victories along the way.

So What Does All This Mean?

There is direct evidence in my life today of the result of Mrs. Ackerman's focus on quality and depth of character in her passion for teaching. Allowing literature to touch your soul compels you to develop a deep sense of empathy. Walking around in others' shoes; seeing the world through their eyes; imagining their perspective and their feelings and their challenges; making better decisions because of that empathy: I attribute that—or at least some of the seeds for it in me and the thousands who have had her as a teacher—to *English Is Life* and Mrs. Ackerman.

And what a needed gift that has been in my life. It got me through the long heartache of losing my father, who had been my truest and best friend in my youth. It allowed me to see the hurt in others and want to help them, too. It has enabled me to find true love in my wife and to gain perspective by seeing myself through her eyes, and it has allowed me to see the world through the eyes of my spirited daughters, who still think of me as Superman, even as they will soon seek independence more than my approval. And, finally, empathy has allowed me to bond with and seek to understand the world through the lens of my son's eyes, compelling me to help him not let autisim and other special needs define him, but rather to find the happiest and best version of himself.

If I've indulged too much in telling my story rather than Mrs. Ackerman's, it is only because I want to show how much impact she continues to have on my life decades after I attended Cold Spring Harbor High School. As a teacher, she was brave and empathetic and demanding, steering us all towards authenticity, depth of character, and, ultimately, joy. *English Is*

Life altered my path as a fourteen-year-old, and now, at 48, it continues to be a guiding principle in my life.

Brian Foerster, a Boston College graduate, is an investment strategist who writes extensively on the financial markets. He lives in New Jersey with his wife and three children; he and his wife are actively involved with organizations that advocate for special needs children and autism education.

∽ *Looking* ℃

ALISSA BOSHNACK BERNSTEIN, CLASS OF 2002

"Look at each other," Mrs. Ackerman told us from the first day of school until the last, teaching us that when we spoke in class we should direct our responses not to her, but to each other instead. This was the most important lesson I learned in my ninth grade English class. What was important was learning, learning from everyone. And looking.

So I watched my classmates. I watched my classmate who often misbuttoned his shirts and was usually buried in a novel while others were gossiping and socializing. In this class, he became a leader, guiding group discussions about the symbolism in *Lord of the Flies* and posing thought-provoking questions that we all eagerly debated. I watched another classmate who typically hid behind his shaggy hair and sat slumped at his desk to avoid participating. But in Mrs. Ackerman's class, he captured everyone's attention. He turned a seemingly insignificant role in *Twelve Angry Men* into a transforming moment, reading the part of one of the jurors with an astonishingly perfect mid-European accent. I watched in awe as his entire body became the part, and we all begged him to do more.

Mrs. Ackerman's insistence that we "look at each other" was not much different from the philosophy of another character we studied that year: Atticus Finch in Harper Lee's *To Kill a Mockingbird*. "You never understand a person until you consider things from his point of view—until you climb into his skin and walk around in it," Atticus told his children. I have kept this lesson at the forefront of my mind from the time I was a teenager in Mrs. Ackerman's class through today, as a lawyer and a new mom in my mid-thirties.

During my career as an attorney, I have worked with the criminally accused, wrongfully convicted, and students facing violations of their educational rights. When my clients' most valued civil rights are on the line, learning their story and considering things from their point of view have always been of critical importance. When I am with my clients, I take the time to learn about their experiences, and we look at each other. As a result, I have developed the trust needed for a client to open up about the details of a stabbing he endured while he was wrongfully incarcerated. I have also felt the anxiety of an undocumented student who feared she could not complete college if the government rescinded the Deferred Action for Childhood Arrivals (DACA) program. When armed with the emotion tied to my clients' personal experiences, I have been able to advocate persuasively for their interests in court.

When I became a new mom to my baby boy, Alexander, I reminded myself of the lessons I learned in Mrs. Ackerman's class. To understand Alexander's needs, I have spent more hours than I could have imagined looking at him. By doing so, I have learned how to take on my most important role. I have learned how to be his mother.

Alissa Boshnack Bernstein, an attorney, is currently the Director of the Center for Public Service Law and an adjunct professor at the Benjamin N. Cardozo School of Law. She is married and has a two-year-old son.

～ *Understanding Who I Am* ～

BRAD KERNER, CLASS OF 1994

Beginning Creative Writing class with the reminder to *Find Your Ness* painted across the ceiling left a lasting impression on me and helped me understand that I could be true to myself, even when it was outside the norm.

While she was inspiring creativity in our writing by disrupting the boundaries and rules of our confined worlds, Mrs. Ackerman was teaching us to know ourselves, be authentic, and create our own boundaries, in which we felt safe exposing who we were. It took me all semester to understand what she meant, but when I finally did, a spark was ignited. She pushed the limits of my growing confidence and motivated me to submit my writing to the school's literary magazine, *Grok*. Looking back, it seems almost silly, but at the time, seeing my writing published and distributed throughout the school seemed to be the carefully orchestrated confidence builder I needed.

Reflecting on the semesters spent in Creative Writing and the extra hours Mrs. Ackerman spent listening to and encouraging me outside of class time, it is easy to see how the threads of her influence are interwoven in my life today. I can truly say that once I found my voice in her class, it stuck, and I have maintained the ability to believe in my gut instincts and know what is right. With this, with the comfort of understanding my *Ness*, I have charted a non-traditional career that I love, focusing my energy on a life of service, starting with the Peace Corps and evolving into a long career with Save the Children. As I travel in and out of different cultures in Africa and Asia, the comfort I have with myself, and the ability to see that the "rules" are different for every individual I interact with, have made working with marginalized people around the world fascinating and fulfilling.

While I now have a successful career, making that first choice to go into the Peace Corps was not easy. I like to think that my experiences in Mrs. Ackerman's class helped me to be comfortable creating the rules that seemed right for me.

Brad Kerner lives in Fairfield, Connecticut, with his wife and three children. When not traveling around the world for work, he spends his time gardening, beekeeping, and blogging on Instagram @myplasticfreefamilyfeud about how his family has learned to lower their waste and its impact on the earth.

~ Wings from Roots ~
Reflections on H-17

Chirag Badlani, Class of 1999

The ceiling of H-17 drew me in first. It was covered in quotes written on construction paper—some of which I knew, some of which I thought I knew, and, as my four years went on, some of which I learned had a different meaning from what I'd originally thought. And when there was no more ceiling space, we turned to the walls, adding lines from Walt Whitman and William Carlos Williams, politicians and poets, teachers and students. I was in that room for freshman English and four years of Speech, Creative Writing, and our literary magazine *(Grok)* meetings after school, and for extra Speech practices—both as the newcomer learning to enunciate and emote, and the captain teaching others to enunciate and emote in their own unique ways. In that room, I delivered a speech for the Ninth Grade Speak-Off about imaginary friends, and I developed real friendships that transcended what high school friendships are *supposed* to be. And when I'd look down from the ceiling or turn from the walls, there was Mrs. Maureen Ackerman, our teacher in every sense of the word.

In H-17, we learned the fundamentals of language and the technical tools we needed to write properly. Sometimes we had to memorize things—speeches and poetry and passages from Shakespeare, portions of which I can still remember. But parsing parts of speech and memorizing stanzas were not archaic teaching tools to Mrs. Ackerman; they were ways to become familiar enough with words to really use them as they were intended to be used. We had to ensure that what we were saying had structure and movement.

And to be performers or orators, we had to be fully present when speaking, enough to move others by letting them actually hear us. Although this may sound insignificant, to this day, when I speak publicly, some in the audience thank me for projecting or using the microphone effectively. When that happens, it occurs to me that many people didn't have a Mrs. Ackerman to tell them this essential aspect of being heard.

Perhaps "being heard" is what was special about H-17 and Mrs. Ackerman's teaching style. She did not view us merely as teenagers. To her, we were capable of creativity, of using words in ways that adults could not (or would not) use. We could study the masters of language and emulate them, or we could take excerpts from comedians and reinterpret them. Through Mrs. Ackerman, we learned that our own words had real power, and that our interpretations of the words of others were valid. Through the study of words and how to say them, we could grow and cultivate the gifts of language and speech that our species was given.

I also recall that H-17 was special at cultivating relationships. Older students with a better ear for language would be mentors. We would support each other at readings, critique each other's speeches and writings, and lend each other books. At the end of Creative Writing class, we had to bring a guest and write about that guest. My sister, who was graduating and leaving for college, and I were fighting at the time, and I brought her as my guest. I wrote a "sestina" about our childhood and her going off into the world. We made up. H-17 could even mend family spats.

What guiding principles or themes remain for teachers and

students and classrooms? I am not a teacher, and I have not been a student in some time. But I suspect that one principle is trust. Students must trust that there are reasons for memorizing, revising, revising again, and then revising once more. They must trust that the poets of whom they had never heard are worth trying to understand. They must trust that their fellow students can have wisdom beyond their years. Teachers must trust that their students are capable, that students have points of view worth exploring, and that while teachers may not reach everyone, there are a few who will grow beyond expectations.

Another theme is storytelling. In a time where we reduce narratives to talking points, telling a story—and teaching how to tell a story—must endure. In H-17, we recognized good storytelling, heard it in others, imitated it, and developed our own ways of telling stories. We read classic stories in English class and performed new plays in Speech. I still reach for this ability to tell an effective story—as a lawyer reminding a judge about my clients' particular stories, as a citizen advocating for the causes I care about, or even as a singer performing lyrics. Stories are what connect me to my listener. Good teaching is good storytelling.

We laid our roots in H-17, and by learning to trust and to take part in the essential human activity of telling stories, we used our wings to go into the larger world outside that room, looking back every so often to remember.

Chirag Badlani, an attorney living in Chicago with his husband and young son, attended Yale University and NYU School of Law. Recognized by peers in "Rising Stars for 20-21," he focuses his professional life on civil rights, employment and immigration law, and supporting organizations that advance justice.

⁓ *A Grateful Parent* ⌐

WARREN KOSTER, PARENT OF CSH STUDENTS

I guess I *do* believe that we are, in so many ways, the stories we tell," an extraordinary woman and teacher wrote in a journal she gave me in April 1998.

I met Maureen Ackerman, the Speech coach, in the fall of 1994 because my son decided he no longer wanted to play football. When I asked why, he sensibly replied that he didn't like to hit people and didn't like people hitting him. Instead, he pursued Speech and Debate, where he concentrated on extemporaneous speaking, and I attended his tournaments for the next four years.

As anyone who has ever attended Speech and Debate tournaments knows, they last all day and have considerable downtime. It was during these lulls that Maureen and I began to know each other, but our bond was irrevocably formed when she learned about the twenty-eight journals I have kept since August 4, 1992, writings that have provided a way to maintain my equilibrium as I both vent my frustrations, impatience, anger, and disappointments, and record the joys of my life and family.

Over time, including when my other son was in her ninth grade English class, Maureen and I talked about everything, but our focus was parenting and teaching. I still remember sitting at a tournament with her on the marble floor of Jamaica High School in Queens, New York, deep in conversation. I learned to be a better parent by listening to her thoughts on reaching her students. Each student was unique to her, just as each child is different to a parent. I quickly realized that teaching and parenting have deep structures in common. Maureen thought it was crucial for teachers to *study* their students, to see each one as more than just a collection of file material. Do this, she believed, and you can discover the key to unlocking a student's passion for learning. She challenged her students, including my sons, by discovering who they were and what they loved. She approached them without ego. Her teaching was never about her. It was always about the students.

Maureen was passionate about so many things, and she wanted you to share her joys. I could see her light up when she discussed her favorite poems and poets, but she must have noticed my blank stare when she talked about them. I had never been exposed to the subject during my own schooling, and, of course, she wanted to remedy that situation. She couldn't bear the thought of going through life without the joy of poetry, so she gave me a volume of poems entitled *Fathers: A Collection of Poems*. I tried my best to feel what she felt and to appreciate the beauty of the words, but after 20 years, I've made my way through only 34 of the collection's 218 pages. I often think if I'd been introduced to poetry earlier in my life by a teacher like Maureen, the result might have been very different. Still, I was fortunate to have spent time with her, and I'm grateful for the journal she gave me. We are, indeed, the stories we tell.

Warren Koster, an attorney, is the managing partner of Koster, Brady, and Nagler, LLP. He and his family live in Lloyd Harbor, New York.

~ *An Inspirational Space* ~

OLIVIA RACANELLI, CLASS OF 1999

There was a time when we were all feeling tired, and Mrs. Ackerman told us to run outside and spin our arms, shouting a line from one of her favorite poems. I remember that kids in other classrooms could see us, and that somehow we didn't care.

It's amazing that we didn't care about the gaze of our peers watching us do something that looked insane: watching us *enjoy* school and English class. H-17 was such a respite from the insecurities of adolescence that it didn't matter if we weren't the cool crowd. To me, we *were* cool, but "The Breakfast Club" cool. The times we shared practicing our speeches and reading our poems and listening to each other and spinning our arms were so joyful and true that we felt like the luckiest people in the building.

Mrs. Ackerman was always imploring us to *feel* the words and the stories, to dig deep and consider what the words might mean to the author, how we might all be interpreting those words differently, and why that might be so. And she was always literally diving over her desk to encourage participation and to respond to us, physically reaching to urge us to think deeply, which made the learning that much deeper.

H-17 was an inspirational space where we could nurture our

intellectual curiosity and develop a lifelong love of learning. It provided a springboard for jumping into future studies, careers, or any endeavor with a spirit of seeking: seeking joy, seeking the underlying depth of written works, seeking connection to others around us.

And, in contrast to the seeking, Mrs. Ackerman taught us to appreciate the moment as well. She encouraged love of self and celebrated unique identities so that, in the very narcissistic period of adolescence, we learned respect and admiration for differences, rather than the pursuit of a prescribed gold standard. I remember all the diverse people and personalities she attracted to H-17. It was like walking into a separate sphere brimming with a life and energy that drew us in until it became our own.

Olivia Racanelli lives in Brooklyn, New York, with her husband and two children.

↷ *Then, and Now* ↶

BONNIE CITTERBART LIEU, CLASS OF 2002

As I graduated from college ready to enter the field of
education—something I always knew I had been called
to do—I kept thinking back to my own time in high school
for inspiration, analyzing in which classes I had felt both most
comfortable and most challenged. And in that reflection, I kept
landing on my time in Speech class with Mrs. Ackerman, so I
contemplated what she had done to foster such a nurturing,
yet still challenging, environment. I vowed to internalize and
implement those lessons in my own teaching.

One lesson was about intuition and understanding the
moment. I remembered the day my friend had come into class
upset over something, and after listening to her problem, Mrs.
Ackerman said only a few words: "Go outside and catch leaves."
No comfort, no fake assurances, just the suggestion to go outside
the glass doors and catch leaves, so that's what Alissa and I did.
We caught leaves, watching their red bodies drift out of the late
October sky, and then we came back in, laughing. It took only
a minute, but in that minute, Alissa let go of what had upset her
and shifted right into the necessary work of the class. Sometimes
the moment matters more than the lesson plan, and I hoped

I would know in my own classroom when to let the moment have its way.

Another lesson was about *seeing*. I wanted to see each student for who he or she was and what he or she had to contribute. I thought about how in H-17 we started class in a circle, no one going unseen, and I began arranging my classroom that way, looking every student in the eye and encouraging them to participate, even when they did not always want to. I loathed that type of engagement my first several weeks in Mrs. Ackerman's class, but eventually it was this encouragement from my teacher and classmates that made me feel comfortable. I wanted to make my own students feel valuable so they could speak truthfully in the safe space I had fostered. Remembering how good it felt to belong, I encouraged my students, especially the ones who shrank into their seats during class, to come after school so I could speak with them one-on-one and learn who they were and how they felt as *people*, not just as *pupils*. Once I established these relationships beyond the classroom, I could speak honestly to the kids, even when what I had to say might be hard for them to hear.

I also kept thinking about how to be someone whose passions were contagious. I remember Mrs. Ackerman's eyes as she contemplated the way a sentence was put together, the choice of word an author made, the syntax and grammar that made someone's thoughts become a great speech. It was impossible to escape her love for words, and even though I knew by my teens that I never wanted to be an English or Speech teacher, there were moments in her classroom when I could not help but feel love for the material she shared, simply because of how she shared it. Her words overflowed with excitement, despite the fact that most high school students or even adults would probably never share that they enjoyed grammar or syntax! I hope as I have taught about the ways the topography on a map influenced the movement of troops across borders during World War II, or I have shared oral histories from the Civil Rights era, I have brought history alive for students. Because I was truly excited by what I was teaching and was willing to demonstrate my love, I wanted my students to find freedom in what excited them.

I always thought the highest compliment I could receive was that I was a tough teacher who challenged each student and was not afraid to correct them, but one who they also knew was fair, always supporting them through feedback and true concern. That's who I remember Mrs. Ackerman being, an educator who was not afraid to challenge me, to tell me when and how I could do something better. I knew that each moment of correction was underpinned by deep caring and love, by her understanding that I hadn't yet reached my full capacity and needed to be challenged. In other words, she saw who I really was and who I could be.

And today, even as I've been out of the classroom in a traditional sense for eight years raising my three children, I want them to say that same thing about me as a mother: That they know I love them dearly, and in that love, I will correct them and challenge them, creating space in which they feel safe and vulnerable enough to fail. I desire in so many ways to make sure that my children know that their voices matter, that I encourage them to try new things because they are loved and fully known, and that they know they have freedom to be passionate about that which their desires reveal to them.

I sometimes wonder if, when I do go back into the classroom, I'll still be able to be the teacher I once was. I feel so much more tired these days, divided in my attention. And yet I know that being a parent has also further cemented many of the lessons I've carried with me.

And I know that many of these lessons I learned for the first time in Mrs. Ackerman's classroom.

Bonnie Citterbart Lieu graduated from Princeton University in 2006 with a degree in history and education. She taught high school history for a number of years in Central New Jersey, where she lives with her husband and three children.

∽ Once, Always ↄ

BOBBY SULLIVAN, CLASS OF 1977

There was a song. There is always a song. Nat King Cole: "…there was a boy, a very strange, enchanted boy…"

The lyrics are poetry.

There was a teacher, one who taught as a calling, a vocation, a passion. One who tried to reach through the mist of the boy's adolescent angst to offer the gift of learning, of reaching inside to what really matters.

But the boy wasn't ready. He left the class. The gift was lost. And it haunted him.

The boy was me. The teacher was Maureen Ackerman.

Lyrics again. This time, Dylan: "…but she never escaped my mind…"

I never forgot Mrs. Ackerman, and I longed for another chance to be her student. No internet then, no Facebook, no Google. I couldn't find her, until Jessica Teich wrote her book, and I read it, and Mrs. Ackerman read it, and then we found each other.

I visited Mrs. Ackerman at her idyllic retreat on the shore of our beloved Long Island Sound. After forty years, the boy and the teacher smiled. It was then that I learned of the poems. Her poems. Forty of them, one for each of the years since I'd seen her.

We made plans; we'd stay connected.

But the Universe had its own plan. Mrs. Ackerman, or Mausie as her friends call her, was visited by cancer.

Things happened quickly. The poems needed to be shared with the world. She had never published them, despite the urging of pre-eminent writers. I was determined to help get her poetry into print.

And I needed to provide her the gift of each moment in the form of a wristwatch. The face of the watch has no numbers or hands, just the word NOW.

The watch is never wrong. It tells us all we need to know.

Mrs. Ackerman, Maureen, Mausie.

She wears the watch. Everyone who sees it on her small wrist is witness to the power of her spirit and the beauty of her soul. She has been living and going with the grace of her words, her poetry now alive and immortal in *This Going, This Grace*.

I read these poems daily. I learn from them. I cherish them as I cherish her.

It is never too late.

Bobby Sullivan lives with his wife, Kandy, on the shore of Cold Spring Harbor. His days in retirement are filled with sailing, fishing, swimming, music, and reading.

∽ Creating What Can Be ⌒

WILLIS GAY, CLASS OF 1990

Schoolwork had always been hard for me. Assignments were simply tasks to complete in order to get where I wanted to go. Finish the reading. Write the paper. Take the exam. Try for an A. My goal was college, and in my mind, there were certain "necessary evils" I needed to endure to get there, including getting good grades. My plan as I entered high school was to hold my nose and get the schoolwork done.

That's about the time I stepped into Maureen Ackerman's ninth grade English class. Mrs. Ackerman wasn't holding her nose. Far from it, she was totally engrossed in what she was teaching. She wasn't getting something done because she had to. She was completely engaged, not only academically, but also emotionally. And her engagement wasn't limited to the material she was teaching. She was also deeply invested in all of us, her students.

The material itself didn't come naturally to me, but from my first moments in Mrs. Ackerman's classroom, I was excited by her interest in what she was teaching and in each of us. It was incredibly energizing. Suddenly, writing assignments were no longer a task to be completed. They became a chance to discover how well I could communicate. Required reading ceased to be something to knock out. Instead, I was curious to find out if the words on the page could make an impression on me like the impact they made on her. I was 15 years old, and for the first time, I was focused on what I was doing instead of what my grade would be.

I changed during ninth grade English. I learned about five paragraph essays, gerund phrases, and adjective clauses, and through learning about Mrs. Ackerman, I also learned about myself. Her values, mood swings, energy, and excitement all affected me. They became a part of me.

Skills I learned in that classroom have, time and again, helped me to connect with people. I learned to communicate authentically and openly. I discovered the value of unabashedly showing others—from business partners to the girls on my daughter's lacrosse team—when I am excited about something. Assignments in Mrs. Ackerman's class and ever afterward in life were no longer chores to be checked off a list. I'm forever grateful to her for opening my eyes…to what could be.

Willis Gay graduated from the University of Pennsylvania in 1994, and now works in the insurance industry. He lives in Westport, Connecticut, with his wife and three children.

⁓ H-17: The Stuff of Possibility ⌒

STEWART GRACE, CLASS OF 2001

Fitting, perhaps, that I'm writing in a journal given to me by Mrs. Ackerman (MA, affectionately, for me) some twenty years ago, because of its significance as the cornerstone of where I really began to write.

What do I remember? I remember the way it felt to step inside H-17. I remember sitting in Mrs. Ackerman's classroom—*our* classroom—on the very first day of ninth grade English class. I remember my rigid combination of a desk/chair facing outward, the large floor-to-ceiling glass doors that slid out onto the back clearing of the school, and the tangled woods beyond.

I remember that Mrs. Ackerman was talking, and that when she walked in front of me, she looked directly into my eyes... and stopped. True, I was more than a little embarrassed and surprised when she said something about my eyes to the entire class—something about Leonardo DiCaprio, who had just recently starred in Baz Luhrmann's modern interpretation of *Romeo and Juliet*.

But she *saw* me. And she asked every single person in that room to really see me, too. We spent the next nine months in that room seeing each other, and—at the very least—learning (or, maybe, practicing how) to try.

My gut tells me there is very little I can remember of the day-to-day. No activity or slice of busy work that somehow made that class comparable to any of the others in my high school years. There were only the things we read together, and the things we wrote together. I remember *Romeo and Juliet* (I still have the balcony scene—well, Romeo's part, at least—memorized by heart to this day). I remember *To Kill A Mockingbird*. I remember *Twelve Angry Men*.

And I remember writing our own speeches, presenting them to a room full of our peers, and even grading each other's final performances. We knew those grades stuck, so we took our task seriously—and our feedback even more so. In a way, I suppose we took our responsibility of grading each other as seriously as we took all our assignments. If we weren't accurate in our grading, there was no question that we might have to justify ourselves at any moment—and no doubt that, provided those justifications were valid, our scoring would be fully supported by Mrs. Ackerman. And I suppose we accepted the task because we knew, deep down, that each of us really did yearn to improve, and that we wanted the truth from each other—not just from a teacher or an adult.

There were no worksheets or onerous scaffolding of our tasks—or at least none that were memorable. There was simply a space in which you were expected to see and be seen; to listen and be heard; to be and let be. Being unprepared for that class was equivalent to not being present—as if you had simply neglected to show up as your true self, even if that truth was the admission that you had arrived unprepared...and thus limited your ability to be present for every other person in the room that day.

As a high school English teacher myself, I struggle daily with what it means to be a teacher for my students. The temptation and, occasionally, pressure to fill learning spaces with quantitative evidence of that very "learning" can seem greater than they have ever been, and many current students' transactional approach to school is strikingly contrary to the environment where H-17 inhabits my memory. There is nothing about the learning in Mrs. Ackerman's classroom that translated to a grade. Time, space, individuality, and content are what mattered.

Having taught at the high school level for only five years, I realize that there simply hasn't been enough time for some groundswell of students to come back and express to me what's worked. Still, there are a few who return, even a handful whom I never formally taught in a course. For each of them, it seems to be the details of the space that mattered most: an adult who was *available*, the door open, the seating open, the conversation open.

Because it's these things I remember, and these things I strive to create in L-506 (my "H-17") each day:

- What it felt like to walk into a room where every individual was valued.
- What it felt like to receive a teacher's unconditional regard.
- What it felt like to be loved and respected by an adult who was not family—at least, not the genetic or domestic kind.
- Feeling that whatever immense possibility this person saw in me *must* have a modicum of truth—and the least I could do was to live my way into that possibility.

In our classroom, there was no more or less each day than what we created there. Mrs. Ackerman was more than a mere guide who made that room safe for our creations; she was a force through which we believed and embraced our own responsibilities as co-creators of that story and space.

If H-17 was possible, it was we who were the stuff of possibility.

Stewart Grace currently teaches English at Sacred Heart Cathedral Preparatory in San Francisco. He has a B.A. in English and Creative Writing from the University of Virginia, as well as a Masters in English and Ph.D. in Literature and Creative Writing from the University of Southern California.

⁓ *What Is the Story?* ᢏ

Rachel Sherman, Class of 1993

How Do I Begin?

I am sitting on a table at the back of the classroom, and two
boys (one I spend afternoons imagining walking with me on the
lacrosse field towards my home and talking about books) stand in
front of me. Everyone is close, and Mrs. Ackerman, my English
teacher, is at their side.

I have just finished reading my most recent poem (is it the
infamous pantoum, "P is for Prozac"?), or is it a story I'm reading
(about a girl who walks on the lacrosse fields with a certain
boy, talking about books and their shared sadness...?), and Mrs.
Ackerman looks at me the way she does sometimes, almost teary,
her bright blue eyes both smiling and touched. She often touches
her heart with her hands, tilting her head sideways. Whenever I
read my work, I look up for her approval. Today I stare up at her,
and now the two boys standing in front of me. I can feel my legs
tingle from sitting too long with my feet dangling.

It is after class, but the boys are there, Mrs. Ackerman catching
them right before they leave. I look down, ready to go to Math or
Science or another class I will undoubtedly fail. Mrs. Ackerman
says, "Read it again. Boys: Listen."

Beyond the space and endless time those years pounded upon

me, it was the fact that Mrs. Ackerman was oblivious to (or perhaps chose to ignore) the eye-rolling that the boys were clearly doing inside their heads. I was a sad girl, always writing, staring, dark, withdrawn, but I found a space between Mrs. Ackerman's hands and heart.

When I finish reading, she gasps, smiles, looks at the boys. "Boys!" she says. "Wasn't that beautiful?!"

Mrs. Ackerman wants them to feel the things she feels. I feel those things. I still do…

WHAT ARE THE STAKES?

The days are bad, long, driving back and forth to therapy in Roslyn, smoking cigarettes by the gym doors. My mood does not lift, does not take me away from my carpeted bedroom, but my stagnancy lets me simmer.

It is a strange stagnancy, one that I actually miss sometimes. It is from within the soup of misery that I write, forgoing everything else that might move me forward. I always have ideas for new stories, dark and obvious but with a hint of something else that Mrs. Ackerman points to with her smile, her gasp, her clasped hands, her eyes.

This day is bad and Mrs. Ackerman offers me a break and a lunch. I am surprised by the stick-shift that she drives, this unexpected power she has. Outside our world she orders a salad at the diner. She complains for me when the waiter brings my onion soup plastic-wrapped and microwaved over.

Mrs. Ackerman sits across from me, asking me questions, letting me speak. I cannot see myself through her eyes, I can only see her in one of her flowy dresses, dresses with blue flowers, or pink. It feels like a secret, knowing how fast she drives her car…

WHAT ARE THE OBSTACLES?

Things look different. Changed. I find boys who let me place my forehead on their shoulders, who yawn while I read them my stories.

Things are different. I win a writing contest, and then another, and the science teacher who told our class that I was destined for Burger King no longer holds first place. I smoke cigarettes and dream of my future apartment filled with sex and ashtrays.

But nothing great happens a third time unless it's fake, and I begin to make the mistakes I will continue making. But I am protected, thought of, remembered. I exist for Mrs. Ackerman, even when I leave the room.

For one of the contests, we go to Washington, D.C. and Mrs. Ackerman comes, too. I shake Bill Clinton's hand and turn to watch as he talks to the blonde girl behind me; it's still a few years away from all of that.

Now, Bill Clinton is handsome, smiling, all bright white teeth. On the White House lawn my parents—those immovable blocks of consequences—are so blurry to me, they are hardly there. I spot Mrs. Ackerman in a hat.

I do not look out at the other parents and teachers, or back at the 50 other kids. They are here because they worked hard, studied, and got the highest SATs in all the land. As usual, I am different, failing almost everything but Creative Writing, but somehow standing here.

Despite the chaos, the clapping, Mrs. Ackerman is my own horizon line. I look out, overwhelmed, seeking it. I feel none of the pride I should feel. I am angry and sad. I am not made the way I'm supposed to be. Mrs. Ackerman shines.

WHAT IS THE CONCLUSION?

I see hope. It is in the shape of the future Mrs. Ackerman dreams for me. It is beyond the safety of her classroom, the terror of the school outside, the lacrosse fields and grounding, and late nights smoking on my roof.

There is hope. I somehow get into college. Mrs. Ackerman gives me an award at graduation for my writing, and I get "best actress" in our senior yearbook because no one knows what I do, only that I do something.

Mrs. Ackerman sees me. I am not who I am. I am potential, hope, a glorious future. *You will be a writer,* she said.

I slither out of the auditorium, past the wooden rows, and up into the hallway of windows marked with silhouettes of birds so that no real birds fly into them. I pass the library where I spent my lunch period, and the faculty bathroom you aren't allowed in. I open the red doors into the back of the school, but none of the usual smokers are there.

I am done, and I can call it all a memory, but it is the most vivid part of my past. Soon, I will see that within her walls was the safest I would ever feel. Sitting at a desk across from Mrs. Ackerman, the silence after I finish reading my most recent poem.

I write stories about this time, but I leave out the beauty. I save the rage for everyone else in the world, which will turn into sadness if I am not vigilant. I've never written about Mrs. Ackerman; I keep her safe as she kept me, away from the wrath, even if only for the time between bells.

A check-in in the classroom. A wave and a hand on the heart. My horizon line.

Rachel Sherman holds an MFA in fiction from Columbia University, where she currently teaches in the same program. Her first book, The First Hurt (2006), *was named one of the 25 Books to Remember by the New York Public Library and was short-listed for The Story Prize and the Frank O'Connor International Short Story Award; her first novel,* Living Room (2009), *was commended for its "perfect pacing" by* The New York Times Book Review.

∾ *Tending Each Other* ᴄ

MAUREEN SWEENEY ACKERMAN

After I retired, I spent years in workshops at local universities, where I finally began to imagine what my own students had meant about not wanting the school year to end, about wanting to hold on for just a little longer to what they had known. For all those years teaching, I knew my own heart, but not until I sat as a post-grad student after retirement did I quite understand what they had been feeling. Now I know why we danced our joy at June gatherings when school had officially closed. We were celebrating what we had individually become, together, both the students and I.

Because it was together that we had heard our single selves when others spoke, each of us listening to the other's words, yet hearing the sound of our own voices, too, caught as they are in the well of memory and shaped by all we have felt. So it was that when Dennis talked about his brother's death from a car crash; and when Lucy remembered the neglected bicycle against the woodshed in her grandmother's backyard; and when Martin wrote about his loneliness since his troubled sister went to boarding school in Ohio, each of us heard our own story inside. The wonder is not that the particulars of one person's story became different particulars of another's. It is that we felt permission to speak what we knew. It is that we were open enough to listen with our full selves.

"Hope may be the thing with feathers," I'd sometimes tell my students at the start of school, "but September is surely the thing with wings." And there, in H-17, we would discover *our* wings, constructing them out of knowing and tending each other. We became the story we would tell together.

ꙅ Arming Teachers with Love ꙅ

Joanna Novick Schwartz, Class of 2001

One October day, Mrs. Ackerman asked us to follow her outside. We huddled against the brisk fall air and wondered why we had left our classroom. Our teacher had a clear purpose. She faced each of us individually, looked in our eyes, shaped her palms into a heart, and blew the air our way. When we returned to the classroom, she instructed us to quietly, "Write what you caught."

It was the fresh breeze spelling optimism in my teacher that quickly translated to a sense of possibility in my heart. Each of my classmates could have caught anything—knowledge, ideas, success, talents, or all, or none, of the above. As we grew together that year, our teacher reminded us that what we had "caught" was attainable because we believed it was there, carried to our hearts and minds by the air we breathed.

That's what learning looked like in this magical place called H-17, where the words "Find Your Ness," and "English Is Life" were painted in large font across the classroom walls.

We learned love through language, inspired by connection and our collective presence. It was a lesson in being human, a guide for how to navigate the complexities that can come in those turbulent teenage years. I've heard Mrs. Ackerman call her decades of teaching at Cold Spring Harbor High School a love affair. The love she spilled out to us mattered then and continues to matter today.

Imagine classrooms everywhere looking like H-17. In a world in which there's talk of arming teachers with guns, why don't we arm them with love?

Joanna Novick Schwartz began her career as a teacher through Teach for America, then took her experiences into consulting with various organizations at home and abroad. She is a proud mom, wife, and lifelong student.

∽ *Afterword* ᴄ

MAUREEN SWEENEY ACKERMAN

Not even cancer can keep me from the classroom. The student and teacher in me is always reaching in, always reaching out, to the world I love.

Early in 2017, my husband and I decided to sell our home on Long Island, where I'd been teaching since 1966. Everything was simple. The pull of our grandchildren in Colorado had proven stronger than the pull of the tides, and the transition from what I'd known my whole life would be easy to navigate. I'd be running along mountain trails instead of beach sand, but the natural world would still be vast and inviting, and I'd continue to hold to the beauty that nourished my soul. I'd start writing groups; I'd enroll in university courses; I'd join meditation and yoga classes. Nothing except the landscape would change, and I'd have my grandchildren to tuck into bed on sleepover Saturdays.

A brain cancer diagnosis a month before our move changed much of that, but it also led me to the cancer clinic ten minutes from my new home. There, shortly after I arrived, I entered the first-ever Writing with Cancer workshop offered by the hospital, yet another classroom in which I could come alive. I could write, I could respond, I could edit, and empathy and compassion could shape my own stories as other patients revealed theirs.

Has there been a life *before cancer* and a different life *after*? Of course. I can no longer run four miles each day, and my walks and speech patterns are slow meanderings. Words are often buried too deep to recover, and sometimes I think my toothbrush is my pen. Medication gives me mood swings, and I need too many afternoon naps. I stumble. I drink tea with whipped cream. I find hair strands in the freezer. My family worries, then rallies, but the strain is unmistakable. I strain to acquaint myself with the stranger in the mirror.

Would I go backwards, knowing what life has become? Sometimes the past is tempting, but cancer is a teacher, too. It's a reminder to live here in the present, in the right-now moment of being alive.

∽ *Acknowledgments* ⌒

"In me, you will live forever," Jessica Teich wrote in 1973, at the end of eighth grade. She spoke for both of us then, and here we are now, in 2021, collaborating on this book about teaching and learning and love. A Yale and Oxford graduate, a Rhodes scholar, an author, lyricist, and composer, Jessica has not surprised me with her accomplishments. I was, after all, dazzled by the adolescent brilliance that I knew would carry her into worlds far beyond Cold Spring Harbor. What does astonish me, though, is her decades-long devotion to who she and I are together. Without her, this book would not exist. It was Jessica who suggested the project; who contacted former students; who read every essay submitted; who arranged the order in which those essays would appear. Seeing a photo of the broken desk in which I sat every day, she also saw the desk as a perfect cover for the book. Thank you hardly seems adequate, Jessica, but you understand that thank you comes from deep in my heart.

And to the writers whose essays are in this book, I'm in awe of what you have carried with you through the decades since you sat in H-17. As you have written, the lessons learned there were beyond the books; they transcended into the stuff of possibility, into the sense of belonging and the sense of freedom that define our needs as human beings. I thank you for affirming our lives together, for saying no to cynicism, and for rejoicing in the realm of everything the word *yes* implies. This book is yours.

Thank you to Mariah Parker, the designer and graphic artist who imagined the look and feel of this book and patiently responded to the many revisions it has undergone, always focusing on the beauty that these student essays deserve. You, Mariah, deserve credit and gratitude for what you've created, and you have mine, truly. Working with you—knowing you—has been a blessing.

Thank you to May Sun, the talented artist who lent her considerable gifts to the project of creating a book cover, her first; and to Peter Simpson Cook, who helped to realize May's vision.

Thank you to my former colleagues, especially John Healy, who welcomed me as coach of the Speech half of the Speech and Debate team; Ceil Daher, English department chair, and Helen Browne, assistant principal, who listened when I asked that Creative Writing and Speech classes be pass/fail electives; Sandra Waller, Dick Kopp, and the late Ray Forest, for years of comaraderie; and the late Dick Ham, who worked with all of my 9th grade students on their informative speeches, and whose encouragement helped those students perform well beyond their own expectations. And special thanks to Ann Scolnick, Bird Norton, Karen Davis, and Theresa Soltiz Mercer, whose kindness has softened my cancer journey.

Thank you to all the Cold Spring Harbor students, administrators, parents, staff, custodial workers, and cafeteria folks who allowed me to be who I am and to love what I love. Without their support, I don't know how this book would have been possible, which is to say, I don't know how Mrs. Ackerman, the teacher, would have been possible. H-17, its walls and ceiling and safety, would not have been possible, either, nor would the desk on which the students scribbled their goodbyes be the desk at which I'm sitting right now as I scribble my gratitude in pen and ink.

To my own teachers, especially Roger Rosenblatt and the late Maggie Ann, I am eternally grateful that you saw me as a writer.

To friends who have read or listened to these essays with grace and patience, and who have made important suggestions, I thank you and love you. You know who you are.

And to my family—Gary, Danny, Kailee, Hudson, and Everly Ackerman—I offer this book with devotion, love, and forever thanks for your steady encouragement and belief in me. Because of you, I am living this new life with my whole heart. Your love sustains me.

⁓ *About the Teacher* ⚬

Maureen Sweeney Ackerman, a lifelong reader, writer, and runner, and recipient of multiple awards for excellence in teaching, has taught English, Creative Writing, and Public Speaking to high school students. She has been a private writing and speaking coach, a memoir and poetry workshop leader for adults, a featured speaker at national conferences, a freelance editor, and a ghostwriter. Until 2017, she lived on Long Island, where running along back roads and the beach ignited her imagination and gave rise to much of her writing. "I was always collecting images," she says. "I was shaping sentences with my feet. I was crafting paragraphs out of air. I was in love with the world, and I spilled that love onto the page." She and her husband currently live in Denver, Colorado.

This Going, This Grace, her first poetry book, was published in 2019.

Photo by Jeff Shusterman

Made in the USA
Middletown, DE
27 January 2022

59831276R00094